For Ben, not even my wildest
imagination could prepare me
for the joy you would bring to my life.

Imagine

Creating Desserts with Christy Tania

How to Use this Book

This book is split into two sections – basic recipes and advanced recipes – with my story sprinkled along the way. I created this book with the intention to push your imagination and to challenge your idea of what a cake can be. If you are scared or unsure about venturing into the realm of imaginative desserts, I would kindly ask you to put this book down, and come back when you're ready to experiment, to be bold, and to let your imagination run free. If you *are* ready for an adventure, then welcome to the beginning of an amazing journey.

Please also note that all measurements in the following recipes are given in grams, except for the gelatine sheets which are given in number of leaves.

Contents

How to Use this Book	2
Equipment	4
Ingredients	8
A Different Way of Creating – Christy's Story	**14**
Mastering Your Imagination – Basic Recipes	**24**
Mousse	28
Ice Cream	48
Cream	52
Sponge Cake	60
Pastry	68
Crumble	76
Ganache	82
Fruit Jelly & *Coulis*	92
Extras	98
Fast Forward – Christy's Story	**114**
Running with Your Imagination – Advanced Recipes	**120**
Chocolate Tempering	124
Raspberry Mushroom	132
Rat! A Touille!	148
Tropic Thun-Bear	162
Chocolate Excellence	174
Rubik's Cube	188
All Eyes on Me	206
Green-y Smith Apple	222
What's Next – Christy's Story	**238**

Equipment

Here is a list of equipment that you will see pop up throughout my recipes. I will list any special equipment required for each dish, especially the advanced ones, but assume these are the must-have items for all recipes.

Oven

A good oven is going to bake or break your soul when it comes to cake making. A good one is not necessarily an expensive one, and an expensive one is not necessarily a reliable one. I would consider a good, reliable oven as one that has a fan forced feature and even heat distribution. Every oven is different; get to know yours well. Bring it to a candle-lit dinner, drink wine with it, and maybe it will let you in on its deepest secret (which corner is hotter, what is its actual temperature) and it will make your *macarons* come out perfectly every time!

Freezer & Fridge

A lot of desserts need to set. It's something that you can't cheat on. Have you ever eaten a cheesecake that had been rested for just an hour versus one that had been rested overnight? Major difference, right?

A well-circulated fridge and freezer can make that process faster and your dessert last longer.

Trays

A good, heavy tray that fits well into your oven and some trays that fit in your fridge/freezer are crucial. Why a heavy tray, you ask? Have you ever baked a cake and the tray just went twisty inside the oven due to heat? It would most definitely ruin whatever you are baking inside. A heavy tray would do the trick.

To have some that fit in your fridge/freezer is necessary when you want to set some desserts in a silicon mould. This way your desserts will stay flat and won't spill everywhere in your freezer.

Stand Mixer

Invest in a stand mixer that has different attachment offerings, as this will broaden your dessert skills and up the adventure! For example, the SMEG stand mixer has a bowl that allows you to churn ice cream!

I would also advise having multiple stainless steel mixing bowls. This will help you when completing complex recipes, especially ones that call for you to whisk your egg whites and egg yolks separately.

Hand Blender

The hand stick blender is my go-to in emulsifying *ganaches*, as it gives that shiny smooth texture. I also like it for blending glazes as it can take out those pesky bubbles. Believe me, it is a good investment.

Food Processor

A strong food processor is so underrated. I use a Thermomix in my kitchen, but if you have another brand, that's fine too. As long as it is strong enough for you to blitz some nuts and chocolate. This is how I make my chocolate 'paste', literally blitzing chocolate *couverture* into pliable form.

Hand Whisk

Ah, the good old friend. The symbol of my trade, and the bane of my existence at the same time. If I ever see another pastry chef with hand whisk tattooed on them… (inhale … exhale …). However, it is a very crucial tool. I prefer one that has a skinnier handle which allows me to manoeuvre my hand while mixing and folding.

Rubber Spatulas

There is a saying that a pastry chef carries a spatula in one hand and palette knife in the other. I find this to be quite true. Get different sizes of spatula, and grab one that has an overall thick rubber head which can handle anything from folding cold *mousse* to mixing hot custard. The flimsy and thin ones usually can't handle hard jobs like caramel making, and it will tear as you go along, risking some pieces ending up in the dessert.

Palette Knives

In our other hand, we have palette knives. I also have them in different sizes: large ones to spread chocolate and cake batters, and small ones to spread and flatten *petit gâteaux* bases. I am proud to say that I can pick up anything using a palette knife. You can keep your fork, spoon and butter knife. Give me a palette knife and I have a full set of cutlery in one hand!

Thermometer

Get a digital one: don't bother with those manual mercury ones. One with a probe that is attached to a heatproof wire is great, because then you can leave it at the edge of the pan as you are cooking. Dessert making is all about precision. There is a huge difference between 118 degrees and 120 degrees when one is caramelising. Calibrate the thermometer often, too. With a good and reliable digital thermometer, nothing is too overwhelming, not even chocolate tempering.

Digital Scales

Same case as with a thermometer: it's all about precision. I have both regular digital scales and smaller (micro) ones. Measure everything right and you only have to do it once: this is another mantra of mine.

Silicon Mats

They're much safer for the environment, so it's a no brainer. They also work much better than baking paper (in my honest opinion) when we are piping things to be baked or frozen. Silicon simply conducts heat and distributes cold temperature better.

Ingredients

Dairy

I would like to be serious about this one. If you can, grab your best local dairy products, and I guarantee you, you have won some parts of the baking/creating battle already!

Butter

Salted or unsalted? This is a good question. If you only have salted butter in your fridge and you are craving that brownie or cookie or salted caramel, go ahead and bake away. However – if you are making some pastry cream or chocolate *crémeux*, always use unsalted butter.

But one thing's for sure: respectfully, and for the love of all pastry gods, you cannot replace butter with margarine for my recipes.

Full Cream Milk

When my recipe calls for milk, I always use full cream milk. The fat percentage is simply the best for cooking with.

Skim Milk Powder

I use skim milk powder in my ice cream recipes, and it's there 100% for the flavour and texture. Adding skim milk powder to ice cream creates that 'bitey' consistency and luxurious mouth-feel.

Cream (Pouring)

In Australia, this is called 'Pure Cream'. It has a fat content of around 35%, doesn't have any thickening agent added to it, and has a pouring liquid consistency. I use this in my ice cream and sauces, because I am making big batches of them and like to keep the mixture in the freezer for use later. If you are just making small batches at a time, you can skip this requirement and go ahead with your heavy or thickened cream.

Thickened Cream

Usually has around 45–50% fat content. When whipped, this cream is quite stable and will retain its fluffy texture when being folded in. You can whip pouring cream as well, but usually it doesn't hold the whipped texture as well as thickened cream.

Caster Sugar

When my recipes call for sugar, I'm talking about superfine caster sugar (unless stated otherwise). Other kinds of sugar will give different results in terms of fluffiness and texture. Superfine caster sugar is fine enough to dissolve easily, and coarse enough to help those little bubbles in *meringue* hold each other tightly like a pair of floating otters.

Glucose

There are many types of sugar syrups out there – from maple to glucose to golden. Glucose is essential for that soft chewy texture in your ice creams, *coulis*, jams, *compotes* and *ganaches*. It also prevents them from crystallising – we all hate opening a crusty jar of jam!

Dextrose

Usually found in corn and wheat, dextrose component is extremely similar to glucose syrup. When I call for it in a recipe, it is usually in dry powder form. I use it a lot in ice cream because it has anti-freeze attributes like normal sugar (saccharose) and anti-crystallising attributes like glucose, but with a less-sweet flavour profile. Dextrose is also highly soluble, which is great in ice cream where you want to have that completely smooth texture. If you are in a tight spot, you can replace it in equal measure with glucose.

Gelatine

Where do I start on gelatine without sounding like a mad scientist? Gelatine is a type of binding agent. It does the same job as agar-agar or xanthan gum, though each applies differently and would have different texture results and methods. Common, store-bought gelatine is usually animal based: really rich in protein and collagen, but unfortunately not vegetarian or kosher friendly. Fish gelatine exists as well, but it tends to have less gelling power and melts at lower temperatures. My recipes here call for animal-based gelatine, either pork or beef. The recipes also use titanium strength gelatine and are measured in leaves rather than in grams. *Leaves are great because you do not have to worry about the blooming strengths, and they are readily available in most major supermarkets*!

Different types of gelatine have different blooming strengths. The different strengths are ultimately interchangeable in leaf form. Let's say if my recipe is calling for 3 leaves of titanium gelatine, and you happen to have only gold gelatine leaves: don't fret. You only need to take 3 leaves of gold gelatine and the result would be the same. Take the same amount of leaves each recipe calls for regardless of the strength. You will be fine.

The size of gelatine leaves matter, though. The leaves I use are roughly 9 cm x 4 cm. There are some gelatine leaves for domestic use that are half the size; if this is the case, just double the quantity.

Just to make sure that we are on the same page in gelatine leaf measurement, here is the weight by sheet (approximately):

- 1 Platinum = 1.75g
- 1 Gold = 2g
- 1 Silver = 2.5g
- 1 Bronze = 3.5g
- 1 Titanium = 5g

To bloom the gelatine leaves, you just have to soak them in ice water until they are softened. Don't bloom them in warm, or room temperature water: this will make the gelatine dissolve and become unusable.

Once the gelatine softens, use your hands to squeeze excess water out and use it immediately as instructed in the recipe.

Now, if you happen to only have powdered gelatine, you need to have your calculator out.

The table below will help you do your conversion.

So, for example: if you happen to have gold gelatine, you need 7.7 grams of gold gelatine powder for each 10 grams of titanium gelatine my recipe calls for. Don't forget to read the manufacturer's instruction on how much water you need to bloom the gelatine you are using.

	Titanium 120 Bloom	Bronze 140 Bloom	Silver 160 Bloom	Gold 200 Bloom	Platinum 120 Bloom	Beef 250 Bloom	Fish 250 Bloom
Titanium	10 g	9 g	8.5 g	7.7 g	7.1 g	6.6 g	6.6 g
Bronze	11.1 g	10 g	9.2 g	8.5 g	7.8 g	7.3 g	7.3 g
Silver	12.1 g	10.8 g	10 g	9.3 g	8.6 g	8.1 g	8.1 g
Gold	13.0 g	11.7 g	10.9 g	10 g	19.2 g	8.7 g	8.7 g
Platinum	13.9 g	12.5 g	11.6 g	10.8 g	10 g	9.3 g	9.3 g
Beef	14.7 g	13.3 g	12.4 g	11.6 g	10.8 g	10 g	10 g
Fish	14.7 g	13.3 g	12.4 g	11.6 g	10.8 g	10 g	10 g

Vanilla

This is also another thing that you will find in almost all recipes of mine. I love the flavour and I also love the little black specks in my desserts.

There are so many different types of vanilla in the world: you can find vanilla extracts, pastes or the actual pod itself. I love all of them, but would use them all differently. In this book, I use vanilla paste throughout. I believe it has the best economy to flavour ratio compared to using extracts or scraping the pods. I encourage you to invest in some good quality vanilla paste for your baking journey. You won't regret it!

I also write QS (Quantity Sufficient) for all of my recipes that call for vanilla. It is simply because, like all spices, this is a game of preference. I have a knack for adding more vanilla than is needed – to the horror of my finance team (because, ahem, it's not cheap). Some of you are probably not that into vanilla and would like to omit it altogether. You do you! There's no right or wrong. However, (and Luke can confirm this) I am right 99.99% of the time. So yeah ... get that vanilla!

Eggs

In this book, I write all my ingredients (apart from the gelatine) in grams: including the eggs. Dessert is a game of precision, and egg is a very important factor. I often say that it would be easier for me to create dairy-free dishes than egg-free.

Egg helps to bind ingredients, and it creates structure and stability in baked mixture. It also helps to emulsify and thicken *anglaise* and custards, and adds moisture and bounciness in sponge cakes.

For such an important architectural piece in a recipe, I like to be very precise - especially with something like *choux* pastry. Weighing your eggs will save you from dry and flat cake every time! Is it additional work for you? Definitely is. But you know what is a LOT more work? Re-doing everything again because the measurement is not right. Scale the eggs!

Flour and Nut Meals

Most of my cakes are actually gluten-free. A little secret of mine – I am actually gluten intolerant. Clinically diagnosed, had a blood test and all. But yeah, sometimes I love to play with the (stomach) pain and gobble that full-gluten cake anyway. Because of this, I developed my recipes either using gluten-free flour or nut meals, such as almond meal or hazelnut meal. I found that using gluten-free flour in my sponges actually makes them lighter and softer in texture. I also love using nut meals in my heavier baked goods like brownies, pound cakes or crumbles.

Almond and hazelnut meals are my go-to friends when it comes to baking denser cakes. They add toasty, nutty aromas and are just simply the best.

Hazelnut meals come with skin and all, but almond meals come either blanched or unblanched. Blanched almond meal contain no skin and therefore it has the beige uniformity of colour, plus a fine and smooth texture. When you are baking cakes, I don't find baking using blanched or unblanched almond meals creates a big difference in the result. However – and this is the most important takeaway from this passage – always use blanched almond meal when making *macarons*. This one is non-negotiable!

Plain Flour

For cakes that require a thicker form – like *génoise* or chocolate cake – I would use plain flour or all-purpose flour. This type of flour has 9–11 grams of protein per 100 grams. These bake well and have great structural gluten strength that will support the thickness of the cake.

Gluten-Free Flour

The one that I use is a blend of corn, rice and tapioca flour. You can replace this kind of generic blend gram for gram with plain flour, but remember is doesn't have the structural integrity of a full-wheat flour. So, if you need to make a thicker cake, choose a gluten-free flour that contains thickener (usually guar or xantham gum). Avoid buckwheat-based flours, as these are quite drying.

Cocoa

Cocoa is another passion of mine. Understanding the role one magic cocoa bean plays in your dessert can do wonders. It literally opens up the realm of your creation. For me personally, it is one of the most important pillars while creating those gravity-defying, texture-bending, optical-deceiving creations.

Dark Chocolate

Some people assume that the higher the percentage of the dark chocolate, the better the quality. This is true in some cases, but not in all. Just like coffee and wine, the territory where the bean is grown plays the most crucial role in the flavour of the chocolate.

To be considered of the dark chocolate family, it has to be at least 43% cocoa mass (cocoa nibs + cocoa butter), with at least 26% of that mass being made of cocoa butter. A good 72% dark chocolate means 72% of that chocolate weight is made of combination of cocoa nibs and cocoa butter while the remaining 28% is predominantly made of sugar. How that 72% differs from one brand to another depends on the ratio of cocoa nibs (where the flavour comes from) to cocoa butter, and also on the region where the nibs come from which would showcase the terroir profile of the chocolate. This is where the term 'single origin' chocolate came from!

When my recipes call for 58% or 72% dark chocolate, can you use them interchangeably? The short answer is yes, but the result would differ in firmness and texture. My mantra is always: choose good quality ingredients. That way you will have won half of your battle.

Milk Chocolate

Just like dark chocolate, milk chocolate has two main ingredients: cocoa mass and sugar. The difference is the addition of milk powder in the ingredients, which usually makes up between 16% and 20% of the overall weight of the chocolate. My recipes usually use milk chocolate with 42–45% cocoa mass, which is the common range for this chocolate category.

White Chocolate

Is white chocolate considered a chocolate? This is a debate that continues to baffle us; because technically speaking, it is. To be considered white chocolate, it has to have fat content that derives solely from cocoa butter: no other kind of fat is allowed! So, if you grab that 'white chocolate' bar and the ingredients list includes 'palm oil' or 'vegetable oil', then what you are holding is not white chocolate.

For my recipes, I call for that genuine white chocolate. It is made of cocoa butter, milk powder, sugar, vanilla and lecithin (emulsifier). It should have that buttery, dried fruit aroma.

Cocoa Powder

Here is my unpopular opinion: I don't think Dutch cocoa powder is any better than natural cocoa powder. They are just different! Just like the other chocolate forms above, a good cocoa powder should just contain that: cocoa mass. It is basically the most pure and intense form of cocoa nibs.

The difference between Dutch and non-Dutch is just the process. Natural or unsweetened cocoa powder tends to be lighter in colour and more acidic (with a pH between 5 and 6). Dutch cocoa powder is alkalised and has a more neutral pH, which is around 7. When a recipe calls for baking powder which contains acid (like most of mine), Dutch cocoa powder is the go-to. But if the recipe contains baking soda (which is by itself an alkaline), it needs the acid from natural cocoa powder to activate.

When you are making ice cream or custard however, none of this matters. You can change one with the other to your preference of taste and colour.

A Different Way of Creating —
Christy's Story

A Different Way of Creating

From a very young age, I have loved to create things. However, I grew up in a pretty conservative family and attended an established Catholic school throughout my childhood in Jakarta, Indonesia. What was accepted as 'beautiful' was not always for me.

I had my own idea of what was beautiful, creative and attractive, and my own way of making things.

I struggled with other arts and crafts, too. Origami was never my *forte*, because following strict instructions just wasn't in my nature. I could follow the rules to a certain extent, but after that I'd just get frustrated and decide to do things my own way. Most of the time I ended up with something different from what I was supposed to make.

I just thought there must be a different way of creating art that was more fun and more efficient. There was.

Mami, The Sparring Partner

Looking back, I realise that this attitude was what we now call 'attention deficit hyperactivity disorder', or ADHD. Bless my Mami who tried her best to understand why she was saddled by this head-strong, super high-energy trickster as a firstborn. We laugh about it now.

My parents were textile merchants. Papi, my dad, worked in a small warehouse with rolls and rolls of textiles stacked up to the ceiling; he organised stock arrivals and dispatches, issued invoices, and managed drivers and labourers.

Mami, my mum, ran the marketing side of the business. She's the one who decided which patterns to print and which trends to start. My parents travelled to Europe, the US, China and Japan to find the latest print trends and techniques.

Mami is a very elegant woman with a small stature – but cross her at your own risk!

All in all, she is a serious but soft-spoken lady. She is one of six siblings and known for her style. Her nickname from friends was 'Princess Jade.'

So imagine the shock when, out of her, came me.

It goes without saying that Mami is a very strong, competitive person. These attributes translated into her desire for me to be the best I could be in everything I did.

She sent me to paint classes and entered me into competitions. I loved the opportunity to channel my creativity, but I didn't win any prizes.

Mami likes to bake. Once a month at school, the teacher would ask all our parents to make the same dish.

I told you Mami was competitive, right? Well, when we were asked to bring cakes to class, she was in her element and finally had a chance to dominate! Back then, we had to do everything by hand, which included hand mixing. Mami would enlist me in the kitchen to help her. I still remember my tiny hands, furiously cranking the big hand mixer, beating the eggs. When the cake came out of the oven and Mami cooled it down, spread buttercream over the sides and added colourful sprinkles on top, it was the most beautiful thing I had ever seen. I was the *proudest kid* in the class with my cake!

Quarter-Life Crisis

After high school, I decided to apply to Nanyang Business School in Singapore. I was accepted, then graduated, then got my first job at IBM Singapore as a management trainee for Global Business Services. I was good at the job, but I got bored again. When I realised that 'working' was a life-long commitment, it suddenly hit me that I'd have to do this job *every day*. It felt like I was trapped. I needed to challenge myself in other ways.

Cooking and baking blogs were hitting mainstream media and I was captivated by the pictures people were posting – especially the pictures of cake pops, which had become a real trend. I thought to myself, *I can do that*!

At first, I bought a pre-made cake mix from the store and baked little brownies and other creations to bring to work. This reminded me of how happy and proud I was showing off Mami's cake to my primary school class, and how proud she was when I told her that everyone wanted my cake! It had made me happy as a kid, and it was making me happy again.

For the first time in my life, I was *accepted* for my creations. Applauded.

Then one of my colleagues asked me to bake cupcakes for her kid's birthday party and insisted she pay me.

After that, the orders just kept coming.

Not-So-Side Hustling

Quickly after those first few orders, I developed an obsession to master the skill of cake making.

I bought some of the best recipe books. I devoured those French pastry books, picked up a few recipes and merged them together to create something suitable for my 'working canvas'. But I would also watch sculpting videos, painting videos and carving techniques to apply to my creations.

After that, I jumped to the fun parts: making cakes that don't look like cakes or *behave* like cakes. Put simply, I was creating stuff that was representative of myself. Someone wanted me to bake a Darth Vader cake? I got it done, with a working, remote-controlled lightsaber attached. What about an Oscar the Grouch cake that talks? Yes, I can do that!

A carousel Winnie the Pooh Cake that actually spins? A three-tier circus cake balancing on a big ball? A train-track cake with a moving, smoking train made entirely of sugar? Yes, yes, and yes! I did it all.

Eventually, the crazy-but-true thing happened: I was making more money baking cakes than I was as Project Manager at IBM. At that time, I spoke to my mentor at IBM and he told me I had two options. The first was to get my MBA at a reputable university. He said a master's degree would be necessary for me to become a senior consultant.

'Or,' he added 'you could do something about that budding cake-making empire of yours.'

To this day, my dear friend and mentor loves to tell this story to his mentees and colleagues – the one about a young woman he used to work with, who decided to eschew the corporate brick road for a pebblier one in France.

And how she never looked back.

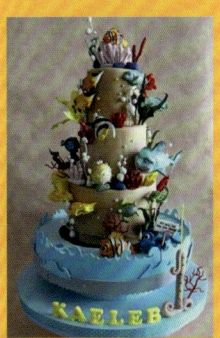
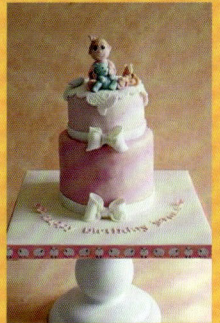

How to Get Lost and Found in France

My approach to the next project in my life was very similar to how I approached cake baking. I was interested in the magic making, the awe inspiring, the delicate wizardry of French desserts that I read and observed while I was training to bake. I understood that if I wanted to level up my edible beauties, I couldn't just teach myself. I needed the foundations. I need the equipment. And most importantly, I needed someone to show me how.

Where could I learn the best French pastry arts and not get bored?

France!

Alain Ducasse, the godfather of culinary schools in France, had recently opened an international pastry course in the small provincial village of Yssingeaux at Haute Loire. It was called ENSP *(L'École Nationale Supérieure de Patisserie)*. It is now part of the larger and super famous École Ducasse institution. If any aspiring pastry chefs ask me where to go to learn the basics of French pastry art, this is my go-to suggestion.

The international course was super new and the students were up-and-coming pastry chefs. Heard of Cedric Grolet? He was *staging* ('interning', in French) in Yssingeaux a little over a decade ago — around the same time I was there.

My parents thought I was crazy, as I already had my career mapped out in front of me and could easily earn more cake-baking money on the side without leaving the comfort of Singapore. But, just like a 100% success rate was not fun in baking, I knew I could not settle for 'easy' in life. Plus, it was France! I yearned for somewhere new.

I found myself being completely immersed in Yssingeaux. That town was so tiny and, apart from the kebab shop and a couple of small restaurants, *nothing* was open after six pm. Not even the convenience stores.

Nevertheless, I thoroughly enjoyed the experience.

I came to that little town to learn about sugar art, chocolate making and the magic of pretty dessert creations. Instead, I fell in love with French desserts and Yssingeaux's charming lifestyle completely. The respect and intricacy of centuries-old methods, coupled with this *laissez faire* way of living was like a beautiful, curated but controlled chaos!

Of course you'll fall in love, I thought to myself. Believe me, you'll fall in love with something if you go to France. You'll fall in love with the town, or the culture, or the food, or the way of life, or perhaps with yourself … or with someone else.

But romance was the last thing in my plan, and the last thing on my mind.

There is Only One 'The Ritz'

If you ever speak to someone from Paris and tell them you've been to or stayed at the Ritz, they will straight up ask you, *'Où?'*/Where?'

If your answer is anywhere on this planet apart from *'Paris'*, then expect a nose scrunch followed by, 'There is only one *Le Ritz!*'

Back at ENSP, our course required us to go for a minimum one-month *stagiaire*, which is a sort of work placement/internship arrangement.

Most of my peers asked to be placed in really cool, artisanal boutique shops. Sébastien Bouillet, Eric Kayser, Arnaud Larher, Victor Hugo, Des Gateaux et du Pain – just to name a few.

In my case, for all the subjects we were taught, I was most intrigued by plated desserts. The pressure to plate perfectly in a timely manner with all those fiddly temperature components? I loved it! I wanted to learn more about plated desserts, but I also liked those precious *petit gâteaux*. Where could I learn about the entire 360 degrees of the pastry world here in France?

My teacher asked me, 'Want to try the Ritz? We can make some calls, but we can't place you there like we do for your friends. You'll have to go, attend the interviews, and hopefully they'll see something in you.'

Yep. Interviews. *Plural*. Also, *in French*.

I took a five-hour train ride to Paris. I arrived late at night and had already booked myself into a small motel at Trocadero at the butt of the Eiffel Tower. This was the part my parents didn't know about, because there was no way in hell that they would've approved of me – a twenty-five-year-old woman – arriving in Paris, alone, in the dead of night. I bought McDonald's (or *'MacDo'* in French) for dinner and checked in to the dingy motel.

I brought with me a thick, heavy laptop and connected to the motel's internet. The entire night, I Google Translated every possible question the interviewer could ask. 'Why do you want to work here?' 'Why do you think you are good for this role?' 'Why pastry?' And then I Google Translated my answers. I memorised them all, even practicing the accents.

The following day, I arrived at the Ritz. I remember I wore black leggings, flats and a cream shirt I bought from H&M. Instantly I regretted it. The guy next to me was interviewing to be a housekeeper and he arrived wearing a suit, tie, briefcase and all. I just sighed, 'Welcome to Paris,' under my breath.

Long story short, my Google Translated questions came up, and I was ready with the Google Translated answers.

Fake it 'till you make it, right? I did five rounds of interviews, from the HR team, to the Head Pastry Chef, to the Exec Head Chef, to the final one: the General Manager.

I will never forget the room with plush carpets, a wide wooden table, tall bookshelves and tall windows overlooking Place Vendôme. The General Manager was tall, lanky and had the warmest smile, perfected by his years in hospitality. He greeted me, read my resume and asked, 'Christy, *parlez-vous anglais?/ do you speak English?*'

I blinked and answered, 'Yes, of course.' And he laughed and spoke in the heaviest American accent, 'Ah! I miss speaking English! I've interviewed so many people today, all in French, and my brain needs a bit of a break.'

There you go. Of course, I got the job in the end.

I started on the night shift, which involved preparing *petit fours* desserts for the restaurant and room service. They attributed my quietness to my being Asian instead of my having *zero* understanding of what was actually going on.

Eventually, I got pretty quick at the job and finished everything before the scheduled time. So, I asked what else I could do. They would tell me, and I would blink back at them in confusion.

This is where the fun started, as they realised that they'd been duped: this newbie couldn't actually speak French and knew very little about French pastries (yet).

If you have watched Hell's Kitchen with Gordon Ramsay, imagine it dubbed in French. I got some pretty angry screams directed at me. In French. I had a chef yell at the back of my head. In French.

One day, I decided I'd had enough of being yelled at. I looked straight at the sous-chef, and told him in English, 'I want to help. I want to learn. Help me to help you!'

He was shocked by this pushback. He stormed out of the kitchen. He returned after smoking a cigarette, put on his apron, and just went, 'Christy! Come here!' *In English!* I came over and he placed multiple bowls in front of me, next to a piece of paper.

'Write! *Crème pâtissière!*'

Then he tore the paper into pieces, wrote down the ingredients in French, and put each of the papers into their allocated bowls. In his super limited English, he explained to me what needed to be done. No one had any idea how grateful I was to Yann for what he did that night. It was the beginning of my impromptu language lessons at the Ritz.

Boredom and Curiosity are Blessings

After a while, I started to get bored again (noticing a pattern here?). I would eye the pretty *petit gâteaux* in the trolley, waiting to be brought up to Bar Hemingway, whenever I came in at the very end of the day shift. The day shift was like a completely different planet for me. Different people, different methods and different outputs.

I was *also* curious about this guy I had met a while back at school.

Remember when I went for my initial interview at the Ritz? After I was done, this guy I'd just met at school – Luke – texted me, 'How was the interview? Do you want to grab pizza when you're back and tell me about Paris?'

I went to grab pizza with him. I told him everything about the Ritz, the pastries I ate while I was there, the beauty of Paris, and he just stared back at me with these brown eyes full of awe. One thing that stoked my interest for him was his curiosity – his hunger to learn about pastries was so intense and pure. He got super excited talking about the skills, flavours, and textures involved in pastry art. He came from a tiny town back in regional Victoria, Australia and told me how he got the money to study in France by opening the right suitcase on *Deal or No Deal*. His eyes sparkled when he spoke about his dog Murphy.

He was super easy on the eyes, too, which made it difficult not to get drawn in.

Luke ended up in Paris as well. He got a job at a traditional German-French pastry shop and, after work, he would bike around Paris and tell me about the sights – things I had missed out on during my first three months of living there, as I was working like crazy.

Have Your Cake and Eat It, Too

If there is anything I learnt in France about life, it's to treat everything like a piece of cake. The French take pastries super seriously; it's an art, but it's also something to enjoy, regardless of the occasion. It could just be because it was Tuesday and we felt like having some. 'Cake is life' is not an overrated term. Cake *does* make your life more enjoyable.

It's all about having your cake and eating it, too.

After I'd spent some time there, the Ritz was preparing for massive renovations, and Luke's visa was also about to expire.

I could find another job in Paris; with my resume I was sure it wouldn't be too hard. I had developed so many transferrable skills and I felt like I only scratched the surface. There was so much more I could learn from great pastry chefs around the world.

I looked into Luke's brown eyes as he cheekily asked me, 'Want to come with me to Australia? Victoria is the largest wine-producing state, and you love your wine …'

Maybe I could have my cake and eat it, too?

Luke told me Victoria is the centre of the greatest sport in the world – Australian football. He told me about the stars back at his countryside home that shine even brighter than those I admired back at Yssingeaux.

He told me there are many restaurants that would *love* to have me as a pastry chef.

One night in Paris, a very drunk friend asked me what my plan was after France and if I would stick with Luke. I laughed and told him I didn't know, but what was important for me was the chance to continue honing my pastry skills. He replied with, 'Pffft … a cake is a cake, but what if that guy turns out to be the father of your children? What's more important than that?' I just smiled, sipped my wine and looked over at Luke, who was debating some football stuff with his fellow Aussie mate on the balcony.

Yeah, I thought, *what if?* Imagine what I'd be missing.

24

basic recipes

Mastering Your Imagination
Basic Recipes

Creating a dish, for me, is like composing music: to do so, you need to understand your chords. *How you* decide to compose your music – or create your dessert – is up to you. The basic recipe section is made up of of those chords: these recipes here are the building blocks of your spectacular creations – *only you* can imagine what you will create. Scattered throughout this book are some sample creations that I have invented by mix-matching these basic recipes with each other to inspire you.

If you looked at my own recipe books that I use to create, they would look very similar to this section. I never create the look of the dish and then develop the recipes: the process isn't linear. Each time I'm creating something, from simple to gravity-defying, I sketch the look that I'm after, brainstorm the flavour and texture that I want, and then go to my recipe books to see what kind of recipes could support this vision. It's never a straight line between concept and creation: just like composing music, it's a dance between yourself and your creations. But if you truly understand your basics, your foundations, then you can be the master of your imagination.

Please note that all measurements in the following recipes are given in grams, except for the gelatine, which is given in a quantity of sheets/leaves. QS stands for Quantity Sufficient – the amount for these ingredients is up to your taste!

Mousse

Tip: For some of my *mousse* recipes – especially ones that include cooking egg yolks in *anglaise* or custard – I would recommend placing some mixing bowls in the freezer ahead of the cooking process. If you have stainless steel bowls, these would be best for this purpose. This material allows the *anglaise* or custard mixture to drop in temperature quickly, allowing you to move on to next step promptly. Cold, stainless steel bowls also reduce the possibility of bacteria growing, and will lengthen the lifespan of your *mousses* … if you can resist finishing them in one go, that is.

vanilla
mascarpone
mousse
(page 41)

dark
chocolate
crémeux
with egg
(page 57)

plain
sponge
(page 64)
soaked in
espresso

Coconut *Mousse*

375	Coconut Cream/ *Purée*
30	Water
105	Sugar
56	Egg Whites
280	Thickened Cream (semi-whipped)

4 *Sheets of Gelatine Leaves*

Method

1. Pre-soak gelatine in ice water. Once bloomed, squeeze to drain excess water. Set aside at room temperature.

2. Heat coconut cream or *purée* on the stove at medium heat. Bring this to a simmer (don't let it boil!), then add bloomed gelatine and whisk gently with hand whisk until all the gelatine is dissolved. Set aside at room temperature.

3. Place egg whites in the bowl of a stand mixer. Use a whisk attachment and start mixing at low speed.

4. At the same time, place water and sugar in a saucepan and heat on the stove at high heat. Place a candy thermometer in the saucepan.

5. Once the thermometer reads 110°C, increase the speed of the stand mixer to high.

6. Once the thermometer reads 118°C, take the saucepan off the heat and tap carefully on the bench to stop bubbles from forming.

7. Reduce the speed of the stand mixer to medium.

8. Once the saucepan syrup becomes clear, carefully pour it at a slow stream into the egg whites in the stand mixer (still whisking on medium). Be careful not to pour the hot sugar syrup onto the moving whisk: drizzle it between the moving whisk and the wall of the mixing bowl.

9 Once all the hot sugar syrup is poured, increase the speed of the whisk to high and continue whisking until stiff *meringue* forms and the mixture cools to room temperature.

10 In a big mixing bowl, add ⅓ of the *meringue* and ½ of the warm coconut cream and gelatine mixture. Use a hand whisk to carefully fold them together.

11 Add another ⅓ of the *meringue* and the other ½ of the warm coconut cream and gelatine mixture. Continue whisking slowly.

12 Add the final ⅓ of the *meringue* and whisk until there are no meringue lumps in the mixture.

13 Check the temperature of the mixture. Once it is under 40°C, fold in the whipped thickened cream with a rubber spatula.

14 Pipe or mould immediately, as the *mousse* will set once cold.

Raspberry *Mousse*

250	*Frozen Raspberries*
250	*Raspberry Purée*
140	*Sugar*
40	*Water*
74	*Egg Whites*
374	*Thickened Cream (semi-whipped)*

4 Sheets of Gelatine Leaves

Method

1. Pre-soak gelatine in ice water. Once bloomed, squeeze to drain excess water. Set aside at room temperature.

2. Heat raspberry *purée* on the stove at medium heat. Bring this to a simmer (don't let it boil!), then add bloomed gelatine and whisk gently with a hand whisk until all the gelatine is dissolved.

3. Pour warm mixture over frozen raspberries and use a hand mixer to blend until smooth. Set aside at room temperature.

4. Place egg whites in the bowl of a stand mixer. Use a whisk attachment and start mixing at low speed.

5. At the same time, place water and sugar in a saucepan and heat on the stove at high heat. Place a candy thermometer in the saucepan.

6. Once the thermometer reads 110°C, increase the speed of the stand mixer to high.

7. Once the thermometer reads 118°C, take the saucepan off the heat and tap carefully on the bench to stop bubbles from forming.

8 Reduce the speed of the stand mixer to medium.

9 Once the saucepan syrup becomes clear, carefully pour it at a slow stream into the egg whites in the stand mixer bowl (still whisking on medium). Be careful not to pour the hot sugar syrup onto the moving whisk: drizzle it between the moving whisk and the wall of the mixing bowl.

10 Once all the hot sugar syrup is poured, increase the speed of the whisk to high and continue whisking until stiff *meringue* forms and the mixture cools to room temperature.

11 In a big mixing bowl, add ⅓ of the *meringue* and ½ of the warm raspberry mixture. Use a hand whisk to carefully fold them together.

12 Add another ⅓ of the *meringue* and the other ½ of the warm raspberry mixture. Continue whisking slowly.

13 Add the final ⅓ of the *meringue* and whisk until there are no *meringue* lumps in the mixture.

14 Check the temperature of the mixture. Once it is under 40°C, fold in the whipped thickened cream with a rubber spatula.

15 Pipe or mould immediately, as the *mousse* will set once cold.

Dark & Milk Chocolate *Mousse*

90	Thickened Cream
90	Milk
QS	Vanilla
45	Sugar
56	Egg Yolks
100	Dark Chocolate (72%)
250	Milk Chocolate
770	Thickened Cream (semi-whipped)

1 *Sheet of Gelatine Leaves*

Method

1. Pre-soak gelatine in ice water. Once bloomed, squeeze to drain excess water. Place in a bowl together with dark and milk chocolate, then set aside at room temperature.

2. Heat thickened cream, milk and vanilla in a saucepan on the stove at medium heat.

3. At the same time, in a separate bowl use a hand whisk to beat egg yolks and sugar vigorously until well combined.

4. Bring the thickened cream, milk and vanilla mixture to a simmer (don't let it boil!), then take the mixture off the heat. Pour ½ into the egg yolks and sugar mixture and hand whisk until well incorporated. Pour this mixture back into the saucepan with the other ½ of the thickened cream, milk and vanilla mixture, and place back on the stove.

5. Mix continuously using a rubber spatula until the mixture reaches 85°C. Then remove from the heat.

6. Immediately pour the hot mixture over the soaked gelatine and chocolate. Blend with a hand blender until smooth and glossy.

7. Pour into a cooled mixing bowl to bring the temperature down quickly. Then, put this in the fridge to bring the temperature down further to 40°C.

8. Pipe or mould immediately, as the *mousse* will set once cold.

Dark Chocolate (72%) *Mousse*

90	*Thickened Cream*
90	*Milk*
QS	*Vanilla*
45	*Sugar*
56	*Egg Yolks*
350	*Dark Chocolate (72%)*
770	*Thickened Cream (semi-whipped)*
1	*Sheet of Gelatine Leaves*

Method

1. Pre-soak gelatine in ice water. Once bloomed, squeeze to drain excess water. Place in a bowl together with dark chocolate, then set aside at room temperature.

2. Heat thickened cream, milk and vanilla in a saucepan on the stove at medium heat.

3. At the same time, in a separate bowl use a hand whisk to beat egg yolks and sugar vigorously until well combined.

4. Bring the thickened cream, milk and vanilla mixture to a simmer (don't let it boil!), then take mixture off the heat. Pour ½ into the egg yolk and sugar mixture and hand whisk until well incorporated. Pour this mixture back into the saucepan with the other ½ of the thickened cream, milk and vanilla mixture, and place back on the stove.

5. Mix continuously using a rubber spatula until the mixture reaches 85°C. Then remove from the heat.

6. Immediately pour the hot mixture over the soaked gelatine and chocolate. Blend with a hand blender until smooth and glossy.

7. Pour into a cooled mixing bowl to bring the temperature down quickly. Then, put this in the fridge to bring the temperature down further to 40°C.

8. Pipe or mould immediately, as the *mousse* will set once cold.

Caramel Milk Chocolate *Mousse*

150	Sugar
300	Thickened Cream
120	Egg Yolks
700	Milk Chocolate
700	Thickened Cream (semi-whipped)

3 *Sheets of Gelatine Leaves*

Method

1. Pre-soak gelatine in ice water. Once bloomed, squeeze to drain excess water. Place in a bowl together with milk chocolate, then set aside at room temperature.

2. Heat thickened cream, milk and vanilla in a saucepan on the stove at medium heat. Bring this to a simmer (don't let it boil!), then take off the heat. Set aside.

3. At the same time, in a separate saucepan caramelise the sugar on medium heat until it reaches a deep amber colour.

4. Pour warm thickened cream, milk and vanilla mixture over the caramel to deglaze it. Continue cooking mixture at a low heat until all the caramel dissolves into the mixture.

5. Place egg yolks in a separate mixing bowl. Pour ½ of the caramel liquid over the egg yolks and hand whisk until well incorporated. Pour this mixture back into the saucepan with the other ½ of the thickened cream, milk and vanilla mixture, and place back on the stove.

6. Mix continuously using a rubber spatula until the mixture reaches 85°C. Then remove from the heat.

7. Immediately pour the hot mixture over the soaked gelatine and chocolate. Blend with a hand blender until smooth and glossy.

8. Pour into a cooled mixing bowl to bring the temperature down quickly. Then, put this in the fridge to bring the temperature down further to 40°C.

9. Fold semi-whipped thickened cream through the mixture using a rubber spatula.

10. Pipe or mould immediately, as the *mousse* will set once cold.

Fraisier (Strawberry & Cream)

fresh strawberries

basic recipes

Fraisier (Modern)

vanilla *mousse* (page 40)

strawberry *coulis* (use recipe for raspberry *coulis* on page 95, replacing raspberries with strawberries)

Vanilla *Mousse*

330	*Milk*
QS	*Vanilla*
60	*Sugar*
25	*Cornflour*
67	*Egg Yolks*
300	*Thickened Cream (semi-whipped)*

2 *Sheets of Gelatine Leaves*

Method

1. Pre-soak gelatine in ice water. Once bloomed, squeeze to drain excess water. Place in a bowl and set aside at room temperature.

2. Heat milk and vanilla in a saucepan on the stove at medium heat.

3. At the same time, in a separate bowl, use a hand whisk to beat egg yolks, cornflour and sugar vigorously until well combined.

4. Bring the milk and vanilla mixture to a simmer (don't let it boil!), then take mixture off the heat. Pour ½ into the egg yolks add sugar mixture and hand whisk until well incorporated. Pour this mixture back into the saucepan with the other ½ of the the thickened cream, milk and vanilla mixture, and place back on the stove.

5. Mix continuously using a rubber spatula until the mixture reaches 85°C. Then remove from the heat.

6. Immediately pour the hot mixture over the soaked gelatine. Blend with a hand blender until smooth and glossy.

7. Pour into a cooled mixing bowl to bring the temperature down quickly. Then, put this in the fridge to bring the temperature down further to 40°C.

8. Fold semi-whipped thickened cream through the mixture using a rubber spatula.

9. Pipe or mould immediately, as the *mousse* will set once cold.

Vanilla Mascarpone *Mousse*

120	*Egg Yolks*
80	*Water*
250	*Sugar*
QS	*Vanilla*
500	*Mascarpone*
500	*Thickened Cream (semi-whipped)*

1 Sheet of Gelatine Leaves (optional)

Method

1. If using gelatine, pre-soak in ice water. Once bloomed, squeeze to drain excess water. Set aside.

2. Place egg yolks in the bowl of a stand mixer. Use a whisk attachment and start mixing at high speed.

3. At the same time, place water and sugar in a saucepan and heat on the stove at high heat. Place a candy thermometer in the saucepan.

4. Once the thermometer reads 118°C, take the saucepan off the heat and tap carefully on the bench to stop bubbles from forming.

5. Reduce the speed of the stand mixer to medium.

6. Once the saucepan syrup becomes clear, carefully pour it at a slow stream into the egg yolks in the stand mixer (still whisking on medium). Be careful not to pour the hot sugar syrup onto the moving whisk: drizzle it between the moving whisk and the wall of the mixing bowl.

7. Once all the hot sugar syrup is poured, increase the speed of the whisk to high and continue whisking until mixture cools to room temperature.

8. Reduce speed to slow, and add in mascarpone and vanilla.

9. Increase speed to medium, continue whisking until mascarpone is well incorporated.

Blackcurrant *Mousse*

500	*Blackcurrant Purée*
40	*Water*
140	*Sugar*
74	*Egg Whites*
374	*Thickened Cream (semi-whipped)*

5 *Sheets of Gelatine Leaves*

Method

1. Pre-soak gelatine in ice water. Once bloomed, squeeze to drain excess water. Set aside at room temperature.

2. Heat blackcurrant *purée* on the stove at medium heat. Bring this to a simmer (don't let it boil!), then add bloomed gelatine and whisk gently with a hand whisk until all the gelatine is dissolved. Set aside at room temperature.

3. Place egg whites in the bowl of a stand mixer. Use a whisk attachment and start mixing at low speed.

4. At the same time, place water and sugar in a saucepan and heat on the stove at high heat. Place a candy thermometer in the saucepan.

5. Once the thermometer reads 110°C, increase the speed of the stand mixer to high.

6. Once the thermometer reads 118°C, take the saucepan off the heat and tap carefully on the bench to stop bubbles from forming.

7. Reduce the speed of the stand mixer to medium.

8 Once the saucepan syrup becomes clear, carefully pour it at a slow stream into the egg whites in the stand mixer bowl (still whisking on medium). Be careful not to pour the hot sugar syrup onto the moving whisk: drizzle it between the moving whisk and the wall of the mixing bowl.

9 Once all the hot sugar syrup is poured, increase the speed of the whisk to high and continue whisking until stiff *meringue* forms and the mixture cools to room temperature.

10 In a big mixing bowl, add ⅓ of the *meringue* and ½ of the warm blackcurrant *purée* and gelatine mixture. Use a hand whisk to carefully fold them together.

11 Add another ⅓ of the *meringue* and the other ½ of the warm blackcurrant *purée* and gelatine mixture. Continue whisking slowly.

12 Add the final ⅓ of the *meringue* and whisk until there are no *meringue* lumps in the mixture.

13 Check the temperature of the mixture. Once it is under 40°C, fold in the whipped cream with a rubber spatula.

14 Pipe or mould immediately, as the *mousse* will set once cold.

Passionfruit & Mango *Mousse*

350	*Passionfruit Purée*
150	*Frozen Mango*
140	*Sugar*
40	*Water*
74	*Egg Whites*
374	*Thickened Cream (semi-whipped)*

4 *Sheets of Gelatine Leaves*

Method

1. Pre-soak gelatine in ice water. Once bloomed, squeeze to drain excess water. Set aside at room temperature.

2. Heat passionfruit *purée* on the stove at medium heat. Bring this to a simmer (don't let it boil!), then add bloomed gelatine and whisk gently with a hand whisk until all the gelatine is dissolved.

3. Pour warm mixture over frozen mango and use a hand mixer to blend until smooth. Set aside at room temperature.

4. Place egg whites in the bowl of a stand mixer. Use a whisk attachment and start mixing at low speed.

5. At the same time, place water and sugar in a saucepan and heat on the stove at high heat. Place a candy thermometer in the saucepan.

6. Once the thermometer reads 110°C, increase the speed of the stand mixer to high.

7. Once the thermometer reads 118°C, take the saucepan off the heat and tap carefully on the bench to stop bubbles from forming.

8. Place the saucepan back on the heat and reduce the speed of the stand mixer to medium.

9. Once the saucepan syrup becomes clear, carefully pour it at a slow stream into the egg whites in the stand mixer bowl (still whisking on medium). Be careful not to pour the hot sugar syrup onto the moving whisk: drizzle it between the moving whisk and the wall of the mixing bowl.

10 Once all the hot sugar syrup is poured, increase the speed of the whisk to high and continue whisking until stiff *meringue* forms and the mixture cools to room temperature.

11 In a big mixing bowl, add ⅓ of the *meringue* and ½ of the warm passionfruit and mango mixture. Use a hand whisk to carefully fold them together.

12 Add another ⅓ of the *meringue* and the other ½ of the warm passionfruit and mango mixture. Continue whisking slowly.

13 Add the final ⅓ of the *meringue* and whisk until there are no *meringue* lumps in the mixture.

14 Check the temperature of the mixture. Once it is under 40°C, fold in the whipped cream with a rubber spatula.

15 Pipe or mould immediately, as the *mousse* will set once cold.

Classic Sundae

fresh raspberries

basic recipes

46

Modern Sundae

- chocolate crumble (page 79)
- vanilla ice cream (page 49)
- chocolate ice cream (page 51)
- raspberry *coulis* (page 95)
- chocolate *crémeux* without eggs (page 56)

Ice Cream

Tip: To make it easier for you to expand your ice cream repertoire, I use a lot of vanilla ice cream as the base and then just add chocolate, coffee, and other simple ingredients to flavour it. I like to make a big batch of vanilla ice cream base, and portion it in ziplock bags at 1 kg each. I then lie them flat in the freezer so they don't take up too much space. When I need to make ice cream, I just defrost a portion or two by putting the bag in a bucket of warm water and then it goes straight in the churner with some flavouring. It's super quick! Dessert for your dinner party: sorted!

Vanilla Ice Cream Base

700	*Milk*
600	*Pouring Cream*
150	*Glucose Syrup*
QS	*Vanilla*
100	*Skim Milk Powder*
88	*Sugar (A)*
48	*Dextrose*
4	*Stabiliser*
88	*Sugar (B)*
264	*Egg Yolks*

Method

1. Heat milk, cream, glucose, skim milk powder, sugar (A) and vanilla on the stove in a large saucepan at medium heat. Bring this to a simmer (don't let it boil!).

2. At the same time, use a hand whisk to mix sugar (B) with the stabiliser and dextrose in a small bowl.

3. In a separate bowl, use a hand whisk to mix the sugar, stabiliser and dextrose mixture and egg yolks vigorously until well blended and pale in colour.

4. Once the liquid in the saucepan is simmering, take off the heat and pour ½ into the egg yolks and sugar mixture. Whisk with a hand whisk until well incorporated.

5. Pour this mixture back into the saucepan with the other ½ of the liquid, and place back on the heat. Mix continuously using a rubber spatula until the mixture reaches 85°C. Then remove from the heat.

6. Pour into a cooled mixing bowl to bring the temperature down quickly. Then, put this in the fridge to bring temperature down to 4°C.

7. Split processed mixture into 1 kg ziplock bags, and store in the freezer until ready to use.

8. Follow the processing instructions for your ice cream churning machine.

Coffee Ice Cream

200	*Vanilla Ice Cream Base*
80	*Instant Coffee Powder*

If you've just finished making the vanilla base, use the warm mixture immediately. If you're taking some vanilla base out from the freezer, defrost it completely before using.

Method

1. Take the warm vanilla mixture and use a hand blender to blend in the instant coffee powder until smooth and glossy.
2. Pour into a cooled mixing bowl to bring the temperature down quickly. Then, put this in the fridge to bring the temperature down further to 4°C.
3. Follow the processing instructions for your ice cream churning machine.

Hazelnut Milk Chocolate Ice Cream

200	*Vanilla Ice Cream Base*
150	*Milk Chocolate*
75	*Glucose Syrup*
100	*Hazelnut Praliné Paste*

Method

1. Take the warm vanilla mixture and use a hand blender to blend in the milk chocolate, glucose and hazelnut *praliné* paste until the mixture is smooth and glossy.
2. Pour into a cooled mixing bowl to bring the temperature down quickly. Then, put this in the fridge to bring the temperature down further to 4°C.
3. Follow the processing instructions for your ice cream churning machine.

Dark Chocolate Ice Cream

800	*Milk*
100	*Pouring Cream*
75	*Glucose Syrup*
45	*Dextrose*
2	*Stabiliser*
40	*Cocoa Powder*
77	*Sugar*
110	*Egg Yolks*
88	*Dark Chocolate*

Method

1. Heat milk, cream and glucose on the stove in a large saucepan at medium heat. Bring this to a simmer (don't let it boil!).

2. At the same time, use a hand whisk to mix sugar with stabiliser, cocoa powder and dextrose in a small bowl.

3. Add egg yolks to sugar mixture and vigorously until well blended and pale in colour.

4. Once the liquid in the saucepan is simmering, take off the heat and pour ½ into the egg yolks and sugar mixture. Whisk with a hand whisk until well incorporated.

5. Pour this mixture back into the saucepan with the other ½ of the liquid, and place back on the heat. Mix continuously using a rubber spatula until the mixture reaches 85°C. Then remove from the heat.

6. Pour hot mixture into a bowl with the dark chocolate and blend with a hand blender until smooth and glossy.

7. Pour into a cooled mixing bowl to bring the temperature down quickly. Then, put this in the fridge to bring the temperature down further to 4°C.

8. Follow the processing instructions for your ice cream churning machine.

Cream

Tip: The major difference between *crémeux* and *mousses* is the consistency. *Mousse* is extremely light and should melt in your mouth, whereas *crémeux* has extra bite and adds intensity to the overall experience. It's also a lot sturdier than *mousse*: if you are making layered cakes, I highly encourage you to try to add *crémeux* that has been chilled overnight between the cake layers instead of buttercream. It's life changing! You can thank me later!

Crème Pâtissière

500	*Milk*
QS	*Vanilla*
125	*Sugar*
40	*Cornflour*
100	*Egg Yolks*
40	*Butter (cubed)*

Method

1. Heat milk and vanilla in a saucepan on stove at medium heat. Don't let this mixture boil.

2. At the same time, in a separate bowl, use a hand whisk to beat egg yolks, cornflour and sugar vigorously until well combined.

3. Once the liquid in the saucepan is simmering, take off the heat and pour ½ into the egg yolks and sugar mixture. Whisk with hand whisk until well incorporated.

4. Pour this mixture back into the saucepan with the other ½ of the liquid, and place back on the heat. Mix continuously using rubber spatula, until the mixture reaches 85°C. Then remove from the heat.

5. Pour mixture over cool, cubed butter, then blend with stick blender until smooth and glossy.

6. Pour into a cooled mixing bowl to bring temperature down quickly.

7. Cover with cling film, pressing down so that the cling film is touching the surface of the mixture all over. Store in the fridge until ready to use.

Chocolate Cake

chocolate *crémeux* with egg (page 57)

chocolate sponge (page 66)

basic recipes

Chocolate Plated Dessert

dark chocolate *mousse* (page 36)

Chocolate *Crémeux* (no egg)

210	*Milk*
240	*Pouring Cream*
QS	*Vanilla*
45	*Glucose*
240	*Dark Chocolate (58%)*
300	*Milk Chocolate*

1 Sheet of Gelatine Leaves

Method

1. Pre-soak gelatine in ice water. Once bloomed, squeeze to drain excess water. Place in a bowl together with dark and milk chocolate and set aside at room temperature.

2. Heat cream, milk, glucose and vanilla in a saucepan on the stove at medium heat until it reaches 75°C.

3. Pour hot mixture into the bowl of chocolate and gelatine. Using a hand blender, blend until mixture is smooth and glossy.

4. Cover with cling film and rest in the fridge to cool down.

5. Mould while in a liquid state and freeze. Otherwise, rest in the fridge overnight and the *crémeux* will become pliable and spreadable – perfect for *macaron* and cake fillings.

Chocolate *Crémeux* (with egg)

265	*Milk*
135	*Pouring Cream*
QS	*Vanilla*
68	*Egg Yolks*
68	*Sugar*
225	*Dark Chocolate (58%)*

1 *Sheet of Gelatine Leaves*

The big difference between this *crémeux* and the one without egg would be the pliability and intensity. This *crémeux* is less brittle and slightly more pliable. It also has a more intense flavour than its eggless counterpart.

Method

1. Pre-soak gelatine in ice water. Once bloomed, squeeze to drain excess water. Place in a bowl together with dark chocolate and set aside at room temperature.

2. Heat pouring cream, milk and vanilla in a saucepan on the stove at medium heat. Don't let this mixture boil.

3. At the same time, in a separate bowl, use a hand whisk to beat egg yolks and sugar vigorously until well combined.

4. Once the liquid in the saucepan is simmering, take off the heat and pour ½ into the egg yolks and sugar mixture. Whisk with a hand whisk until well incorporated.

5. Pour this mixture back into the saucepan with the other ½ of the liquid, and place back on the heat. Mix continuously using a rubber spatula until the mixture reaches 85°C. Then remove from the heat.

6. Pour the hot mixture over soaked gelatine and chocolate, then blend with a hand blender until smooth and glossy.

7. Pour mixture into a cooled mixing bowl to bring the temperature down quickly. Put this in the fridge to bring the temperature down further.

8. Mould while in a liquid state and freeze. Otherwise, rest in the fridge overnight and the *crémeux* will become pliable and spreadable – perfect for *macaron* and cake fillings.

Vanilla *Crémeux*

220	*Milk*
QS	*Vanilla*
55	*Sugar*
15	*Cornflour*
50	*Egg Yolks*
30	*White Chocolate*
180	*Thickened Cream (semi-whipped)*

1 *Sheet of Gelatine Leaves*

Method

1. Pre-soak gelatine in ice water. Once bloomed, squeeze to drain excess water. Place in a bowl with the white chocolate and set aside at room temperature.

2. Heat milk and vanilla in a saucepan on the stove at medium heat. Don't let this mixture boil.

3. At the same time, in a separate bowl, use a hand whisk to beat egg yolks, cornflour and sugar vigorously until well combined.

4. Once the liquid in the saucepan is simmering, take off the heat and pour ½ into the egg yolks, cornflour and sugar mixture. Whisk with a hand whisk until well incorporated.

5. Pour this mixture back into the saucepan with the other ½ of the liquid, and place back on the heat. Mix continuously using a rubber spatula until the mixture reaches 85°C. Then remove from the heat.

6. Pour mixture over gelatine and white chocolate, then blend with a hand blender until smooth and glossy.

7. Pour into a cooled mixing bowl to bring the temperature down quickly. Then, put this in the fridge to bring the temperature down further to 40°C.

8. Fold through semi-whipped thickened cream using a rubber spatula.

Passionfruit *Crémeux*

250	*Passionfruit Purée*
230	*Egg Yolks*
120	*Sugar*
30	*Potato Starch*
250	*Butter (cubed)*

Method

1. Heat passionfruit *purée* in a saucepan on the stove at medium heat. Don't let this mixture boil.

2. At the same time, in a separate bowl, use a hand whisk to beat egg yolks, sugar and potato starch vigorously until well combined.

3. Once *purée* is simmering, take off the heat and pour ½ into the egg yolks, sugar and starch mixture. Whisk with a hand whisk until well incorporated.

4. Pour this mixture back into the saucepan with the other ½ of the liquid, and place back on the heat. Mix continuously using a rubber spatula until the mixture reaches 85°C. Then remove from the heat.

5. Pour into a cooled mixing bowl to bring the temperature down quickly.

6. Add cubed butter to the warm mixture and blend with a hand blender until mixture is silky and smooth.

7. Cover with cling film and rest in the fridge to cool down.

8. Mould while in a liquid state. Otherwise, rest in the fridge overnight and the *crémeux* will become pliable and spreadable – perfect for *macaron* and cake fillings.

Sponge Cake

Tip: Most (if not all) of my sponge cake recipes require you to whip or whisk egg yolk and egg whites separately. If you have 2 stand mixer bowls, this will save you a lot of time. However, if not, make sure you clean and dry the bowl and whisk attachment really well between whipping the egg yolks and egg whites. Fat and water are big enemies; the residue of fat from the egg yolks or the droplets of water from rinsing the bowl prior could cause your *meringue* to not rise properly. So take care! Also, all my sponge recipes can be made gluten-free. Just replace flour at a 1:1 ratio with gluten-free flour that does not include buckwheat. Buckwheat flour is extremely dry and will change the recipe proportions completely. My favourite gluten-free flour is a blend of rice flour, tapioca and maize starch.

Biscuits *à la Cuillère* (Ladyfinger Sponge)

285	*Egg Yolks*
143	*Sugar (A)*
72	*Potato Starch*
143	*Plain Flour*
345	*Egg Whites*
143	*Sugar (B)*
QS	*Icing Sugar for Dusting*

Method

1. Preheat oven to 180°C (fan forced).
2. In a stand mixer bowl, use a whisk attachment to whisk egg yolks and sugar (A) at high speed until pale and fluffy.
3. In another stand mixer bowl, use a different (or completely cleaned and dried) whisk attachment to whisk egg whites and sugar (B) at high speed until stiff peaks have formed. Set aside.
4. In another big bowl, sift together flour and potato starch.
5. Fold ½ of the yolk mixture into the dry ingredients using a rubber spatula until homogenous.
6. Fold in ½ of the *meringue* (egg whites mixture) using a rubber spatula.
7. Fold in the other ½ of the egg yolks mixture, followed by the other ½ of the *meringue*, until well incorporated.
8. Place batter in a piping bag with a large round nozzle.
9. Line a tray with a silicon mat then pipe the mixture onto the paper in straight lines of your desired length.
10. Sift icing sugar generously on top of each piped line.
11. Bake for 10–12 minutes. Leave to cool before using.

Genoise

120	*Sugar*
240	*Eggs*
120	*Plain Flour*
2	*Baking Powder*

Method

1. Preheat oven to 180°C (fan forced).

2. In a stand mixer bowl, use a whisk attachment to whisk eggs and sugar until pale and almost doubled in volume. Set aside.

3. In a separate big mixing bowl, mix and sift all dry ingredients together.

4. Carefully fold ½ of the egg mixture into ½ of the dry ingredients using a rubber spatula until homogenous.

5. Fold in the other ½ of the egg mixture, followed by the other ½ of the dry ingredients until well incorporated.

6. Line a deep tray with a silicon mat and pour in the batter. Spread evenly with a palette knife.

7. Bake for 12–15 minutes or until yellow-golden in colour. Leave to cool before using.

Plain Sponge

91	*Egg Yolks*
80	*Sugar (A)*
330	*Egg Whites*
130	*Sugar (B)*
140	*Gluten-Free Flour*
100	*Vegetable Oil*

Method

1. Preheat oven to 175°C (fan forced).

2. In a stand mixer bowl, use a whisk attachment to whisk egg yolks, oil and sugar (A) at high speed until pale and fluffy. Set aside.

3. In another stand mixer bowl, use a different (or completely cleaned and dried) whisk attachment to whisk egg whites and sugar (B) at high speed until stiff peaks have formed. Set aside.

4. In another big bowl, sift the gluten-free flour.

5. Fold ½ of the egg yolks mixture into the sifted flour using a rubber spatula until homogenous.

6. Fold in ½ of the *meringue* (egg whites mixture) using a rubber spatula.

7. Fold in the other ½ of the egg yolks mixture, followed by the other ½ of the *meringue*, until well incorporated.

8. Line a deep tray with a silicon mat and pour in the batter. Spread evenly with a palette knife.

9. Bake for 12–15 minutes or until yellow-golden in colour. Leave to cool before using.

Chocolate Sponge

195	*Egg Yolks*
169	*Sugar (A)*
195	*Egg Whites*
44	*Sugar (B)*
91	*Gluten-Free Flour*
63	*Cocoa Powder*
63	*Butter (melted)*

Method

1. Preheat oven to 180°C (fan forced).
2. In a stand mixer bowl, use a whisk attachment to whisk egg yolks and sugar (A) at high speed until pale and fluffy.
3. In another stand mixer bowl, use a different (or completely cleaned and dried) whisk attachment to whisk egg whites and sugar (B) at high speed until stiff peaks have formed. Set aside.
4. In another big bowl, sift together gluten-free flour and cocoa powder.
5. Fold ½ of the egg yolks mixture into the dry ingredients using a rubber spatula until homogenous.
6. Fold in ½ of the *meringue* (egg whites mixture) using a rubber spatula.
7. Fold in the other ½ of the egg yolks mixture, followed by the other ½ of the *meringue*, until well incorporated.
8. Add melted butter and fold together until well incorporated.
9. Line a deep tray with a silicon mat and pour in the batter. Spread evenly with a palette knife.
10. Bake for 12–15 minutes. Leave to cool before using.

Joconde (Almond Sponge)

150	*Egg Whites*
35	*Sugar*
210	*Eggs*
150	*Almond Meal*
150	*Icing Sugar*
65	*Plain Flour*
45	*Butter (melted)*

Method

1. Preheat oven to 190°C (fan forced).

2. In a stand mixer bowl, use a whisk attachment to whisk egg whites and ½ of the sugar until stiff peaks form. Set aside.

3. In another stand mixer bowl, use a different (or completely cleaned and dried) whisk attachment to whisk whole eggs and the other ½ of the sugar until the mixture is fluffy and pale.

4. In a separate big mixing bowl, mix all dry ingredients together.

5. Fold ½ of the egg mixture into the dry ingredients using a rubber spatula.

6. Carefully fold in ½ of the *meringue* (egg whites mixture) until homogenous.

7. Fold in the other ½ of the egg mixture, followed by the other ½ of the *meringue* mixture, until well incorporated.

8. Pour in melted butter and fold together well.

9. Line a deep tray with a silicon mat and pour in the batter. Spread evenly with a palette knife.

10. Bake for 14 minutes, or until yellow-golden in colour. Leave to cool before using.

Pastry

Tip: All the plain flour used for my shortcrust pastries can be replaced with gluten-free flour for a delicious gluten-free option. The only recipe you can't substitute for a gluten-free pastry is my *choux* pastry: we need the gluten to hold the puff!

Please see my tips on replacing plain flour with gluten-free flour at the start of the sponge section.

Shortcrust Pastry

250	Plain Flour
94	Icing Sugar
31	Almond Meal
3	Salt
150	Butter (cubed, small)
55	Eggs
QS	Vanilla

Method

1. Preheat oven to 160°C (fan forced).

2. Combine all dry ingredients and butter in a stand mixer bowl. Use a paddle attachment to mix at medium speed until mixture has a sandy consistency.

3. Still mixing, gradually add eggs and vanilla until a soft dough is formed.

4. Use a rolling pin to roll out pastry mixture between sheets of baking paper, creating pastry sheets of roughly 0.5 cm in thickness.

5. Leaving the pastry sheets between the sheets of baking paper, move the pastry sheets onto the tray and freeze.

6. Once frozen, cut the pastry into desired shapes using a knife or cutter. Store in the freezer until ready to use.

7. Arrange pastry parts on a silicon mat and bake for 14 minutes. Leave to cool before using.

Chocolate Shortcrust Pastry

235	*Plain Flour*
15	*Cocoa Powder*
94	*Icing Sugar*
31	*Almond Meal*
3	*Salt*
150	*Butter (cubed, small)*
55	*Eggs*
QS	*Vanilla*

Method

1. Preheat oven to 160°C (fan forced).
2. Combine all dry ingredients and butter in a stand mixer bowl. Use a paddle attachment to mix at medium speed until mixture has a sandy consistency.
3. Still mixing, gradually add eggs and vanilla until a soft dough is formed.
4. Use a rolling pin to roll out pastry mixture between sheets of baking paper, creating pastry sheets of roughly 0.5 cm in thickness.
5. Leaving the pastry sheets between the sheets of baking paper, move the pastry sheets onto the tray and freeze.
6. Once frozen, cut the pastry into desired shapes using a knife or cutter. Store in the freezer until ready to use.
7. Arrange pastry parts on a silicon mat and bake for 14 minutes. Leave to cool before using.

Choux Pastry

63	*Milk*
188	*Water*
100	*Butter*
8	*Sugar*
3	*Salt*
150	*Plain Flour*
230	*Eggs (whisked)*

Method

1. Preheat oven to 180°C (fan forced).

2. In a medium saucepan, combine milk, water, butter, sugar and salt and bring to a simmer on medium heat.

3. Add flour and mix on low heat with a rubber spatula. A light film will form on the bottom of the saucepan. Keep mixing until a ball of dough forms.

4. Scrape the dough into a stand mixer bowl. Use a paddle attachment to mix at medium speed to cool. The dough is cool enough when the mixture has stopped steaming.

5. Once cooled, gradually add eggs until fully incorporated. The mixture should be smooth but still sticky.

6. Place dough in a piping bag with a large round nozzle.

7. Pipe dough onto silicon mat to use immediately. Alternatively, pipe them into small silicon half-sphere mould and freeze. When needed place them on silicon mat and leave for 4-5 minutes to defrost slightly.

8. Once ready to use, place *sablage* on top (if using) and bake at 180°C for 15 minutes Refer to *sablage* recipe, page 104.

9. Without opening your oven, drop the temperature to 150°C and bake for a further 10 minutes until crisp and golden in colour. Do not open the oven until the very end.

10. Take out of the oven and leave to cool before using.

Choux Pastry *Éclairs*

63	*Milk*
188	*Water*
100	*Butter*
8	*Sugar*
3	*Salt*
150	*Plain Flour*
230	*Eggs (whisked)*

Method

1. Preheat oven to 180°C (fan forced).

2. In a medium saucepan, combine milk, water, butter, sugar and salt and bring to a simmer on medium heat.

3. Add flour and mix on low heat with a rubber spatula. A light film will form on the bottom of the saucepan. Keep mixing until a ball of dough forms.

4. Scrape the dough into a stand mixer bowl. Use a paddle attachment to mix at medium speed to cool. The dough is cool enough when the mixture has stopped steaming.

5. Once cooled, gradually add eggs until fully incorporated. The mixture should be smooth but still sticky.

6. Place dough in a piping bag with a large round star nozzle.

7. Pipe dough into long tubes on a silicon mat and freeze. Once frozen, cut dough into either 7 cm lengths (for regular *éclairs*) or 3 cm lengths (for little 'Duchess' *éclairs*).

8. Add sablage on top, then bake at 180°C for 17 minutes. Refer to *sablage* recipe, page 104.

9. Without opening your oven, drop the temperature to 150°C and bake for a further 10 minutes until crisp and golden in colour. Do not open the oven until the very end.

10. Leave to cool before using.

Éclairs Croquembouche

choux pastry (page 72)

sablage (page 104)

chocolate shortcrust pastry (page 71)

passionfruit milk chocolate *ganache* (page 85)

passionfruit *crémeux* (page 59)

basic recipes

St. Honoré

Crumble

Tip: All the plain flour used for my crumbles can be replaced with gluten-free flour for a delicious gluten-free option.

Please see my tips on replacing plain flour with gluten-free flour at the start of the sponge section.

dark chocolate crumble (page 79)

spiced crumble (page 80)

plain crumble (page 78)

Crumble

100	*Butter*
100	*Plain Flour*
100	*Almond Meal*
50	*Sugar*
50	*Brown Sugar*
3	*Salt*
2	*Cinnamon Powder*

Method

1. Preheat oven to 160°C (fan forced).

2. In a stand mixer bowl, use a paddle attachment to mix all ingredients until well incorporated and a pliable dough is formed.

3. Line a tray with a silicon mat. Place a wire rack on top of the tray and press dough through the wire rack to create even pieces. Remove the rack and distribute dough pieces evenly on the tray.

4. Place the tray in the oven for 15 minutes. Then, take the tray out and use a metal scraper to scrape the pieces and roughly chop on the tray.

5. Return the tray to the oven and bake for a further 15 minutes until pieces are golden brown in colour. If they're still pale, bake for another 5–10 minutes.

6. Cool crumble completely at room temperature before using.

Crumble (Chocolate)

100	Butter
100	Plain Flour
100	Almond Meal
50	Sugar
50	Brown Sugar
3	Salt
2	Cinnamon Powder
100	Dark Chocolate (58%) (melted)

Method

1. Preheat oven to 160°C (fan forced).

2. In a stand mixer bowl, use a paddle attachment to mix all ingredients until well incorporated and a pliable dough is formed.

3. Line a tray with a silicon mat. Place a wire rack on top of the tray and press dough through the wire rack to create even pieces. Remove the rack and distribute dough pieces evenly on the tray.

4. Place the tray in the oven for 15 minutes. Then, take the tray out and use a metal scraper to scrape the pieces and roughly chop on the tray.

5. Return the tray to the oven and bake for a further 15 minutes until pieces are golden brown in colour. If they're still pale, bake for another 5–10 minutes.

6. Cool crumble completely at room temperature.

7. Once cooled, fold in melted dark chocolate using a spatula until all crumble pieces are well coated. Spread onto a tray and leave to cool at room temperature.

Crumble (Spiced)

100	Butter
100	Plain Flour
100	Almond Meal
50	Sugar
50	Brown Sugar
3	Salt
2	Cinnamon Powder
80	Milk Chocolate (melted)
3	Ginger Powder
2	Nutmeg Powder

Method

1. Preheat oven to 160°C (fan forced).

2. In a stand mixer bowl, use a paddle attachment to mix all ingredients until well incorporated and a pliable dough is formed.

3. Line a tray with a silicon mat. Place a wire rack on top of the tray and press dough through the wire rack to create even pieces. Remove the rack and distribute dough pieces evenly on the tray.

4. Place the tray in the oven for 15 minutes. Then, take the tray out and use a metal scraper to scrape the pieces and roughly chop on the tray.

5. Return the tray to the oven and bake for a further 15 minutes until pieces are golden brown in colour. If they're still pale, bake for another 5–10 minutes.

6. Cool crumble completely at room temperature.

7. Once cooled, fold in melted milk chocolate using a spatula until all crumble pieces are well coated. Spread onto a tray and leave to cool at room temperature.

Ganache

Tip: All these *ganache* recipes are great for macaron filling when unwhipped. Being unwhipped gives the mixture a chewier and denser texture that you want to have for *macaron* fillings. Unwhipped, *ganache* is also amazing for masking or filling cakes.

When whipped, these *ganaches* can even replace *mousses* if you're after an easier, no-fuss substitute.

Ganache is super versatile, but requires really high-quality chocolate. It's also important to be careful not to overheat the liquid getting poured over the chocolate (if this is boiling, it will burn the chocolate). These things can make or break a *ganache*.

Dark Chocolate (72%) *Ganache*

300	Thickened Cream (A)
350	Dark Chocolate (72%)
150	Butter (cubed)
QS	Vanilla
350	Thickened Cream (B)

Method

1. Heat thickened cream (A) and vanilla in a saucepan on medium heat. Mix continuously with a rubber spatula until the mixture reaches 80°C.

2. Pour hot mixture over dark chocolate, then blend with a hand blender, gradually adding cubes of butter. Mix until smooth and glossy.

3. Add thickened cream (B) and hand blend to combine.

4. The mixture can be used as is for a thicker and chewier consistency. Pour into moulds while warm and freeze overnight, or store in the fridge overnight with cling film pressed down so it is touching the mixture all over. Then pipe for use.

5. If using a whipped mixture, cover mixture with cling film, pressing down so that the cling film is touching the surface of the mixture. Refrigerate overnight.

6. Once set, whip to soft peaks with a hand mixer until the mixture has a *mousse* consistency.

7. Place mixture in a piping bag and use as desired.

Orange & Milk Chocolate *Ganache*

200	*Milk*
350	*Orange Compote*
750	*Milk Chocolate*
225	*Butter (chopped)*

Method

1. Heat cream in a saucepan on medium heat. Mix continuously with a rubber spatula until it reaches 80°C.

2. Pour hot mixture over milk chocolate, then blend with a hand blender, gradually adding cubes of butter. Mix until smooth and glossy.

3. Add orange *compote* and hand blend to combine. Refer to orange *compote* recipe, page 96.

4. Once set, put in a piping bag to pipe onto *macarons* or on top of/between cake layers.

Passionfruit & Milk Chocolate *Ganache*

200	*Passionfruit Purée*
750	*Milk Chocolate*
225	*Butter (chopped)*

Method

1. Heat *purée* in a saucepan on medium heat. Mix continuously with a rubber spatula until it reaches 80°C.

2. Pour hot mixture over milk chocolate, then blend with a hand blender, gradually adding cubes of butter. Mix until smooth and glossy.

3. Once set, put in a piping bag to pipe onto *macarons* or on top of/between cake layers.

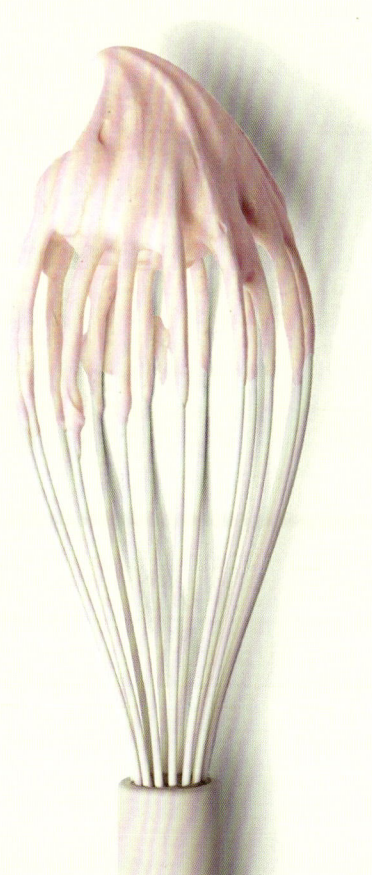

Raspberry *Ganache*

250	*Thickened Cream (A)*
180	*Frozen Raspberries*
150	*White Chocolate*
250	*Thickened Cream (B)*

1 *Sheet of Gelatine Leaves*

Method

1. Pre-soak gelatine in ice water. Once bloomed, squeeze to drain excess water. Place in a bowl with the white chocolate.

2. Heat thickened cream (A), vanilla and frozen raspberries in a saucepan on medium heat. Mix continuously with a rubber spatula until the mixture reaches 80°C.

3. Pour hot mixture over soaked gelatine and white chocolate, then blend with a hand blender until smooth and glossy.

4. Add thickened cream (B) and hand blend to combine.

5. The mixture can be used as is for a thicker and chewier consistency. Pour into moulds while warm and freeze overnight, or store in the fridge overnight with cling film pressed down so it is touching the mixture all over. Then pipe for use.

6. If using a whipped mixture, cover mixture with cling film, pressing down so that the cling film is touching the surface of the mixture. Refrigerate overnight.

7. Once set, whip to soft peaks with a hand mixer until the mixture has a *mousse* consistency.

8. Place mixture in a piping bag and use as desired.

Lemon *Ganache*

300	*Thickened Cream (A)*
100	*Lemon Purée*
160	*White Chocolate*
250	*Thickened Cream (B)*

1 *Sheet of Gelatine Leaves*

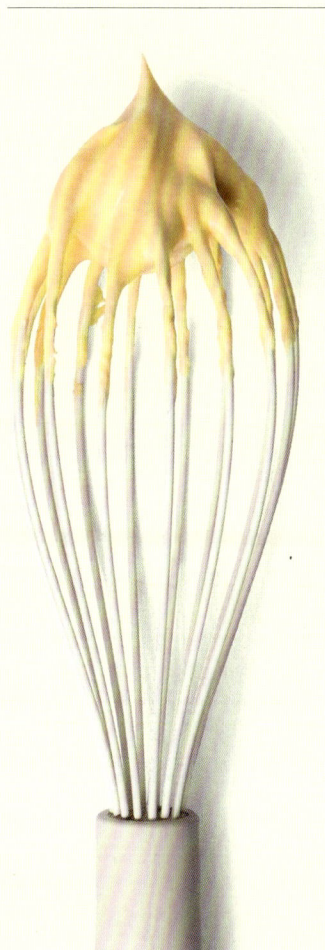

Method

1. Pre-soak gelatine in ice water. Once bloomed, squeeze to drain excess water. Place in a bowl with the white chocolate.

2. Heat thickened cream (A), vanilla and lemon *purée* in a saucepan on medium heat. Mix continuously with a rubber spatula until the mixture reaches 80°C.

3. Pour hot mixture over soaked gelatine and white chocolate, then blend with a hand blender until smooth and glossy.

4. Add thickened cream (B) and hand blend to combine.

5. The mixture can be used as is for a thicker and chewier consistency. Pour into moulds while warm and freeze overnight, or store in the fridge overnight with cling film pressed down so it is touching the mixture all over. Then pipe for use.

6. If using a whipped mixture, cover mixture with cling film, pressing down so that the cling film is touching the surface of the mixture. Refrigerate overnight.

7. Once set, whip to soft peaks with a hand mixer until the mixture has a *mousse* consistency.

8. Place mixture in a piping bag and use as desired.

Lime *Ganache*

380	*Thickened Cream (A)*
170	*Lime Purée*
225	*White Chocolate*
380	*Thickened Cream (B)*

2 *Sheets of Gelatine Leaves*

Method

1. Pre-soak gelatine in ice water. Once bloomed, squeeze to drain excess water. Place in a bowl with the white chocolate.

2. Heat thickened cream (A), vanilla and lime *purée* in a saucepan on medium heat. Mix continuously with a rubber spatula until the mixture reaches 80°C.

3. Pour hot mixture over soaked gelatine and white chocolate, then blend with a hand blender until smooth and glossy.

4. Add thickened cream (B) and hand blend to combine.

5. The mixture can be used as is for a thicker and chewier consistency. Pour into moulds while warm and freeze overnight, or store in the fridge overnight with cling film pressed down so it is touching the mixture all over. Then pipe for use.

6. If using a whipped mixture, cover mixture with cling film, pressing down so that the cling film is touching the surface of the mixture. Refrigerate overnight.

7. Once set, whip to soft peaks with a hand mixer until the mixture has a *mousse* consistency.

8. Place mixture in a piping bag and use as desired.

Coconut *Ganache*

125	*Thickened Cream (A)*
125	*Coconut Cream*
50	*White Chocolate*
125	*Thickened Cream (B)*

1 *Sheet of Gelatine Leaves*

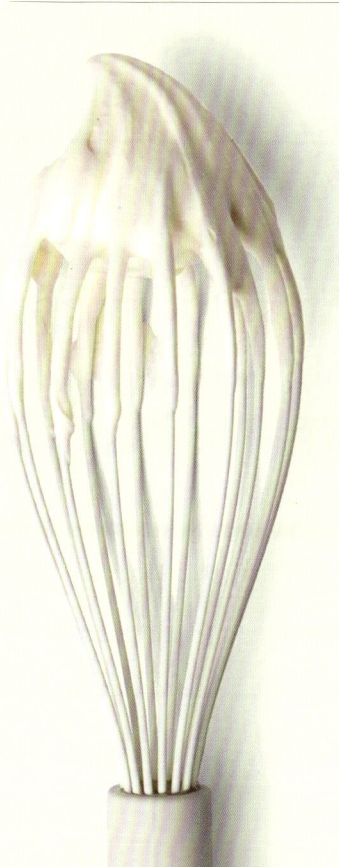

Method

1. Pre-soak gelatine in ice water. Once bloomed, squeeze to drain excess water. Place in a bowl with the white chocolate.

2. Heat thickened cream (A), vanilla and coconut cream in a saucepan on medium heat. Mix continuously with a rubber spatula until the mixture reaches 80°C.

3. Pour hot mixture over soaked gelatine and white chocolate, then blend with a hand blender until smooth and glossy.

4. Add thickened cream (B) and hand blend to combine.

5. The mixture can be used as is for a thicker and chewier consistency. Pour into moulds while warm and freeze overnight, or store in the fridge overnight with cling film pressed down so it is touching the mixture all over. Then pipe for use.

6. If using a whipped mixture, cover mixture with cling film, pressing down so that the cling film is touching the surface of the mixture. Refrigerate overnight.

7. Once set, whip to soft peaks with a hand mixer until the mixture has a *mousse* consistency.

8. Place mixture in a piping bag and use as desired.

Vanilla *Ganache*

312	*Thickened Cream (A)*
170	*Milk*
QS	*Vanilla*
200	*White Chocolate*
313	*Thickened Cream (B)*

2 *Sheets of Gelatine Leaves*

Method

1. Pre-soak gelatine in ice water. Once bloomed, squeeze to drain excess water. Place in a bowl with the white chocolate.

2. Heat thickened cream (A), vanilla and milk in a saucepan on medium heat. Mix continuously with a rubber spatula until the mixture reaches 80°C.

3. Pour hot mixture over soaked gelatine and white chocolate, then blend with a hand blender until smooth and glossy.

4. Add thickened cream (B) and hand blend to combine.

5. The mixture can be used as is for a thicker and chewier consistency. Pour into moulds while warm and freeze overnight, or store in the fridge overnight with cling film pressed down so it is touching the mixture all over. Then pipe for use.

6. If using a whipped mixture, cover mixture with cling film, pressing down so that the cling film is touching the surface of the mixture. Refrigerate overnight.

7. Once set, whip to soft peaks with a hand mixer until the mixture has a *mousse* consistency.

8. Place mixture in a piping bag and use as desired.

Matcha *Ganache*

250	*Thickened Cream (A)*
160	*Milk*
20	*Matcha Powder*
180	*White Chocolate*
250	*Thickened Cream (B)*

2 Sheets of Gelatine Leaves

Method

1. Pre-soak gelatine in ice water. Once bloomed, squeeze to drain excess water. Place in a bowl with the white chocolate.

2. Heat thickened cream (A), matcha powder and milk in a saucepan on medium heat. Mix continuously with a hand whisk until the mixture reaches 80°C.

3. Pour hot mixture over soaked gelatine and white chocolate, then blend with a hand blender until smooth and glossy.

4. Add thickened cream (B) and hand blend to combine.

5. The mixture can be used as is for a thicker and chewier consistency. Pour into moulds while warm and freeze overnight, or store in the fridge overnight with cling film pressed down so it is touching the mixture all over. Then pipe for use.

6. If using a whipped mixture, cover mixture with cling film, pressing down so that the cling film is touching the surface of the mixture. Refrigerate overnight.

7. Once set, whip to soft peaks with a hand mixer until the mixture has a *mousse* consistency.

8. Place mixture in a piping bag and use as desired.

Fruit Jelly & *Coulis*

basic recipes

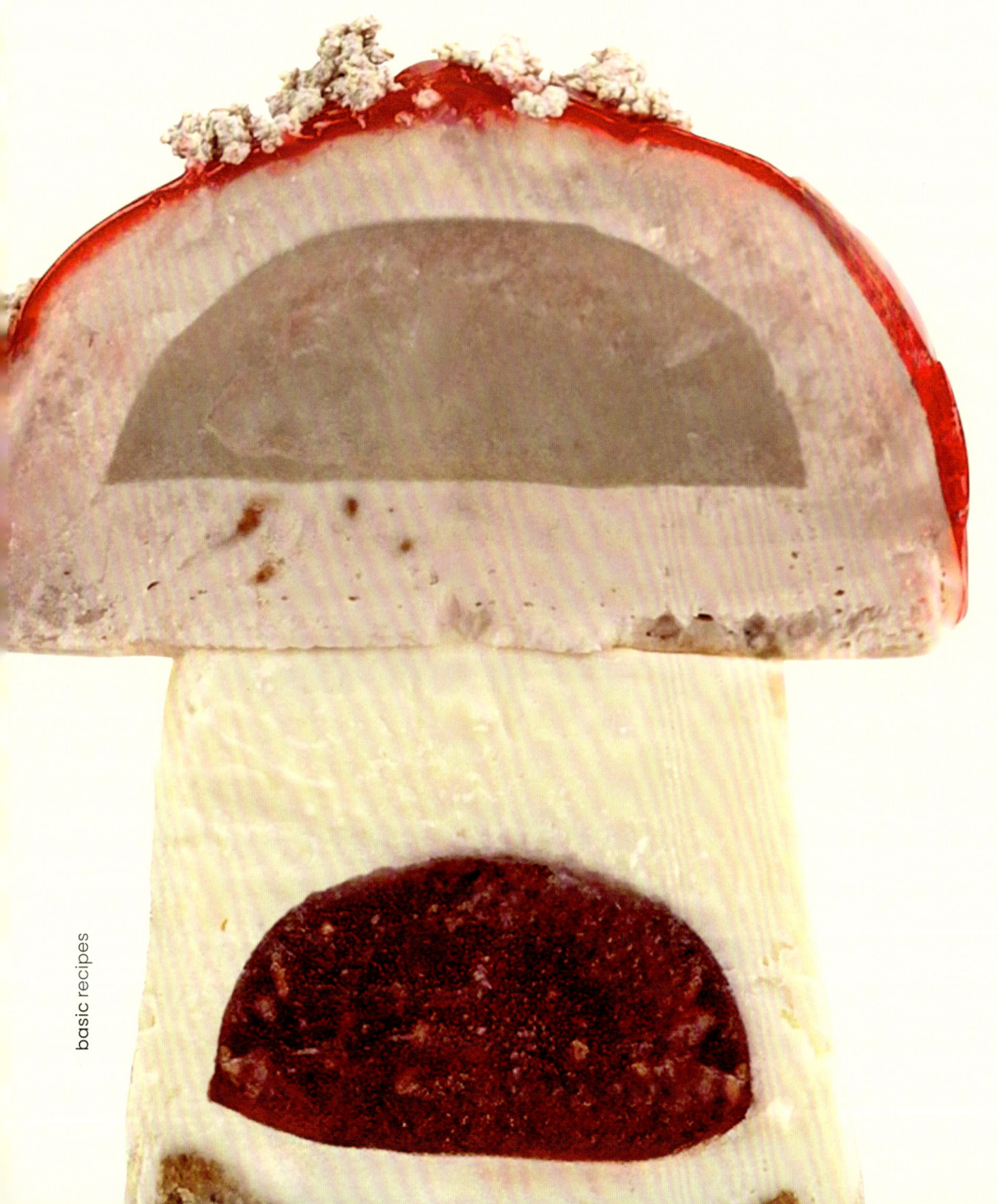

Lychee Jelly

260	Lychee Purée
55	Sugar
30	Glucose

2 *Sheets of Gelatine Leaves*

Method

1. Pre-soak gelatine in ice water. Once bloomed, squeeze to drain excess water.

2. Heat sugar, glucose and lychee *purée* in a saucepan on medium heat. Mix continuously with a rubber spatula until the mixture reaches 80°C.

3. Pour hot mixture over soaked gelatine, and blend with a hand blender until smooth and glossy.

4. Transfer mixture to a cool bowl and let the jelly cool to room temperature before using or decanting it.

Raspberry Jelly

100	Frozen Raspberries
250	Raspberry Purée
40	Sugar
30	Glucose

2 *Sheets of Gelatine Leaves*

Method

1. Pre-soak gelatine in ice water. Once bloomed, squeeze to drain excess water.

2. Heat sugar, glucose, raspberry *purée* and frozen raspberries in a saucepan on medium heat. Mix continuously with a rubber spatula until the mixture reaches 80°C.

3. Pour hot mixture over soaked gelatine, and blend with a hand blender until smooth and glossy.

4. Transfer mixture to a cool bowl and let the jelly cool to room temperature before using or decanting it.

Mango & Coconut Jelly

500	*Mango Puree*
125	*Passionfruit Purée*
125	*Coconut Cream*
125	*Sugar*
150	*Glucose*

8 *Sheets of Gelatine Leaves*

Method

1. Pre-soak gelatine in ice water. Once bloomed, squeeze to drain excess water.

2. Heat sugar, glucose, mango *purée*, passionfruit *purée* and coconut cream in a saucepan on medium heat. Mix continuously with a rubber spatula until the mixture reaches 80°C.

3. Pour hot mixture over soaked gelatine, and blend with a hand blender until smooth and glossy.

4. Transfer mixture to a cool bowl and let the jelly cool to room temperature before using or decanting it.

Coffee Jelly

Tip: espresso can be replaced with instant coffee.

300	*Espresso*
100	*Sugar*
100	*Glucose*

6 *Sheets of Gelatine Leaves*

Method

1. Pre-soak gelatine in ice water. Once bloomed, squeeze to drain excess water.

2. Heat sugar, glucose and espresso in a saucepan on medium heat. Mix continuously with a rubber spatula until the mixture reaches 80°C.

3. Pour hot mixture over soaked gelatine, and blend with a hand blender until smooth and glossy.

4. Transfer mixture to a cool bowl and let the jelly cool to room temperature before using or decanting it.

Raspberry *Coulis*

500	*Frozen Raspberries*
100	*Sugar*
200	*Glucose*

Method

1 Heat glucose, sugar and frozen raspberries in a saucepan on the stove at medium heat and bring to a boil. Mix continuously using a rubber spatula for 3 minutes at a boil.

2 Take off the heat. Blend *coulis* with a hand blender until smooth (be careful of the hot splatter).

3 Pour into a cold bowl. Place cling film over the mixture, pressing down so that the cling film is touching the surface of the mixture. Rest in the fridge until ready to use.

Mango *Coulis*

300	*Frozen Mango*
250	*Mango Purée*
100	*Sugar*
100	*Glucose*

Method

1 Heat glucose, sugar, mango *purée* and frozen mango in a saucepan on the stove at medium heat and bring to a boil. Mix continuously using a rubber spatula for 3 minutes at a boil.

2 Take off the heat. Use a hand blender to blend *coulis* until smooth, being careful of the hot splatter.

3 Pour into a cold bowl. Place cling film over the mixture, pressing down so the cling film is touching the surface of the mixture all over, and rest in the fridge until ready to use.

Orange *Compote*

1000	*Oranges (seedless)*
850	*Orange Juice*
440	*Sugar*
13	*Pectin NH*
QS	*Vanilla*

Method

1. Place the oranges in a big saucepan and fill with water until all oranges are submerged. Place on the stove at medium to high heat. Put a plate on top of the oranges to stop them from floating to the surface.

2. Continue boiling until the oranges are soft. To test softness, prick an orange with the tip of a knife.

3. Drain water from the saucepan. Then add orange juice and vanilla. Use a hand blender to blend oranges, juice and vanilla together. Put the mixture back on the stove and bring to a boil.

4. In another mixing bowl, mix Pectin and sugar. Give mixture a quick stir with a hand whisk to break all lumps.

5. Add sugar and pectin mixture to boiling orange pulps, and mix with a rubber spatula while the mixture boils for 5 minutes.

6. Transfer mixture to a cool bowl and let the *compote* cool to room temperature before using or decanting it.

Extras

Macarons

300	*Sugar*
57	*Water*
100	*Egg Whites (A)*
300	*Icing Sugar (sieved)*
300	*Almond Meal*
100	*Egg Whites (B)*

Tips: For a colourful *macaron*, mix the colour into the mixture at step 2. I always use powdered food colouring, as these are quite intense, a little bit really goes a long way, and it won't alter the consistency of the recipe. If you want to make the colour even more intense, add some food colouring into your sugar mixture at step 1 as well. This will colour your *meringue* and add depth of colour to your almond paste.

'Ribbon consistency' here refers to when you can lift your spatula and let the *macaron* mixture drop back into your bowl in a continuous flow-like 'ribbon' that doesn't break. If the mixture breaks, this means it is underworked. The mixture also needs to be thick enough that it doesn't spread out and revert to a liquid once it touches the base of the bowl. If it does this, it means the mixture is overworked. Underworked mixture will give you brittle, rough-surfaced *macarons*. Overworked mixture will give you flat, uneven and deflated *macarons*. In some instances, underworked mixture is better than overworked mixture; it's best to be vigilant and stop mixing before you take it too far.

99

Method

1. In a food processor, blitz icing sugar and almond meal in quick succession pulses. Do not blitz for too long otherwise the almond meal will start releasing oil.

2. Sieve the almond and sugar mixture into a large bowl, and fold in egg whites (B) with a rubber spatula until a firm paste is formed.

3. While mixing, place egg whites (A) in a stand mixer bowl with a whisk attachment. Start mixing at low speed.

4. At the same time, place water and sugar in a saucepan and on the stove at high heat. Place a candy thermometer in the saucepan.

5. Once the thermometer reads 110°C, increase the speed of stand mixer to high.

6. Once the thermometer reads 118°C, take the saucepan off the heat. Carefully tap saucepan on the bench to stop bubbles from forming.

7. Reduce the speed of the stand mixer to medium speed.

8   Once the hot sugar syrup becomes clear, slowly pour it into the egg whites (B) in the stand mixer bowl (still whisking on medium). Be careful not to pour the hot sugar syrup onto the moving whisk: drizzle it between the moving whisk and the wall of the mixing bowl.

9   Once all the hot sugar is poured, increase the speed of the whisk to high and continue whisking until stiff *meringue* forms and the mixture reaches room temperature.

10 Fold ⅓ of the *meringue* into the almond meal paste using a rubber spatula and mix well. Keep repeating this step until all the *meringue* is used and a 'ribbon consistency' is achieved.

11 Pipe circles of mixture onto a silicone mat and leave to rest for 15–20 minutes while oven is preheating to 150°C (fan forced).

12 Bake for 15 minutes. Take out of the oven and let the *macarons* cool down completely before peeling them off the mat.

13 Pair 2 of the *macarons* together and fill with your desired filling (buttercream, *crémeux* or *ganache*).

102

basic recipes

Sablage

250	*Plain Flour*
250	*Brown Sugar*
200	*Butter*

Tip: For colourful *sablage*, add food colouring powder in step 1. For chocolate-flavoured *sablage*, replace 15 grams of the plain flour with cocoa powder, and add in at step 1.

Method

1   Combine all dry ingredients and butter in a stand mixer bowl and, using a paddle attachment, mix at medium speed until a ball of dough is formed.

2   Use a rolling pin to roll out *sablage* dough between sheets of baking paper, creating *sablage* sheets of roughly 0.3 cm in thickness.

3   Leaving the *sablage* sheets between the sheets of baking paper, move *sablage* onto the tray and freeze.

4   Once frozen, cut *sablage* into desired shapes using a knife or cutter. Store in the freezer until ready to use.

Chocolate Chip Cookie

135	*Butter (softened)*
100	*Sugar*
100	*Raw Sugar*
100	*Brown Sugar*
40	*Hazelnut Praliné (optional)*
QS	*Vanilla*
50	*Eggs (beaten)*
200	*Plain Flour*
60	*Hazelnut Meal*
30	*Almond Meal*
2	*Bi-Carb Soda*
4	*Salt*
40	*Hazelnuts (toasted & chopped)*
30	*Almonds (toasted & chopped)*
175	*Chocolate Chips*

Tip: I use 3 different kinds of sugar because each has a different melting point, giving your cookie excellent crunchiness. If you don't have all 3 different types of sugar, fret not! You can replace all sugar with caster sugar.

I also keep aside some dark chocolate buttons and sea salt flakes. I like (correction, love) to press some buttons onto raw cookie dough balls and sprinkle some sea salt flakes prior to baking the cookies.

I make my own hazelnut *praliné* by pouring equal amounts of hot caramel over hazelnuts, letting the mixture cool and then blitzing it using a food processor. Otherwise, you can buy the regular hazelnut paste from supermarket.

Method

1. Preheat oven to 160°C (fan forced).

2. In a stand mixer bowl with a paddle attachment, mix butter, sugars and vanilla until the formed cream is fluffy and pale.

3. Add hazelnut *praliné* if using and mix through.

4. Add eggs slowly until everything is well combined, and then mix in dry ingredients, followed by nuts and chocolate chips.

5. Let mixture rest in the fridge for 30 minutes to 1 hour.

6. Using an ice cream scooper, scoop the dough to form balls and drop them onto a silicon mat. Flatten them slightly. Press on some dark chocolate buttons and sprinkle sea salt on top if desired (see tips).

7. Bake for 12–15 minutes: 12 minutes will give your cookies chewier insides, and 15 minutes will give them a crunchier texture.

8. Let cookies cool completely before serving.

107

Brownies

610	*Brown Sugar*
488	*Butter (softened)*
390	*Eggs*
269	*Dark Chocolate (58%) (melted)*
220	*Plain Flour*
25	*Cocoa Powder*
3	*Salt*

Method

1. Preheat oven to 160°C (fan forced).

2. In a stand mixer with a paddle attachment, add butter and brown sugar. At a medium to high speed, mix together until a pale and fluffy cream forms, stopping every few minutes or so to scrape the side with a rubber spatula.

3. Gradually add eggs and melted chocolate to butter mixture until well incorporated.

4. Reduce speed of the mixer to medium, then sift in dry ingredients and continue mixing, stopping every few minutes or so to scrape the side until everything is mixed together.

5. Lightly spray a baking tray with oil spray, and then line it with baking paper. Pour mixture onto a tray.

6. Bake for 30 minutes, or until an inserted skewer or toothpick comes out clean. Leave to cool completely on a rack before removing from the tray.

Banana Brownie

90	Brown Sugar
488	Butter (softened)
80	Sugar
135	Eggs
225	Frozen Banana
70	Plain Flour
1	Nutmeg Powder
120	Milk Chocolate (melted)

Method

1. Preheat oven to 160°C (fan forced).

2. Place frozen bananas on a tray lined with a silicon mat. Bake until golden in colour (approximately 15 minutes). Set aside to cool completely, or place in the fridge for faster cooling.

3. In a stand mixer with a paddle attachment, add butter and sugars. At a medium to high speed, mix together until well incorporated and a fluffy cream forms, stopping every few minutes or so to scrape the side with a rubber spatula.

4. With a hand blender, blend eggs and baked banana into a thick liquid. Then gradually add to butter and sugar mixture. Continue mixing until well incorporated.

5. Reduce mixer speed to medium, then sift in dry ingredients and continue mixing, stopping every few minutes or so to scrape the side until everything is mixed together.

6. Pour in the melted chocolate and continue mixing until the batter is smooth.

7. Lightly spray a baking tray with oil spray, and then line it with baking paper. Pour mixture onto a tray.

8. Bake for 15 minutes, or until an inserted skewer or toothpick comes out clean. Leave to cool completely on a rack before removing from the tray.

basic recipes

111

basic recipes

113

Fast Forward —
Christy's Story

Fast Forward...

The year is 2024, and everything that happened between 2020 and 2023 seemed like a combination between the world's cruellest prank and something that only the producers of *The Last of Us* could envision.

The pandemic, just like a thriller movie, really was all about the survival of the fittest. In all aspects. Physical, emotional, and for us business owners? Let's say it was much *much* more than what we bargained for. When Luke and I decided to open a humble pastry shop called 'GLACÉ' back in 2017, we just wanted to have an avenue for people to enjoy our creations while making a decent living at the same time.

The pandemic was earth shattering to all businesses. We were told to 'find new ways to reach your customers'. We were told to 're-think your offerings'. We were told to 'pivot' (damn it! If I hear that word *one* more time...).

All the while trying to make sense of what was going on in the world, trying to protect yourself and your family, while some of us were coping with the fact that we couldn't keep our businesses going.

We did come up with some amazing ideas as a business during this time. We realised that 'this too shall pass'.

In short, we survived the pandemic. As a business, and as a couple. Heck, I was even one of those people that came out of lockdown *fitter*! I spun my stationary bike every day at home to stay sane, and I walked my dogs three times a day so I had reason to get out of the apartment.

At the same time though, there were so many losses.

I lost both my grandma (my mum's mum, my last surviving grandparent) and my aunt (my mum's sister) within six months of each other; and neither my Mum nor our family could be there for the funerals because of the COVID rules.

fast forward – Christy's story

I saw how broken my Mum was and I honestly think she still hasn't recovered from this trauma of losing two of her closest friends and not being able to be there or process it normally (like saying goodbyes, or giving them the last hug before they were gone).

Luke and I had to postpone our wedding. We were supposed to be married in 2020, with my late grandma planning to come. She gave me her cheongsam that she wore to my aunt's wedding thirty years ago so I could wear it during our Tea Ceremony. I did wear that dress to our Tea Ceremony in the end … in 2022.

Our business lost so many staff – staff that were like family to us – because they decided to move back to their home countries.

We also changed focus (gosh, I almost wrote pivoted!) so many times. We tried everything we could to keep the business alive during the pandemic, that we lost vision of who we were for a while. At one point I was selling trays of macaroni and cheese for God's sake! All in the name of survival. But survive we did.

2022-2023

Not only were the lockdowns difficult, but our release back into the wild in 2022 was just as chaotic and crazy! It was an extremely busy year. At the time, I thought it would be the busiest year of my life. Let's just dot-point that year, because everything was a blur.

1. I got married. Three times. *To the same guy.* One civil wedding, one Australian wedding, and one Indonesian wedding. How was the experience of organising three weddings that happened within six months of each other? 0/10, do not recommend.

2. We opened a third and temporary shop in Melbourne airport. We had received the offer before lockdown, and then we had to scramble to organise the logistics in a month.

3. Oh, and I got pregnant.

Now, the last point was the big one for me. I got pregnant bang in the middle of 2023. I was the healthiest I had ever been when I fell pregnant. Definitely way healthier than most other thirty-six-year-old women out there. I took pride in that. So surely, *surely*, I would get to have one of those healthy, glowing pregnancies all those influencers portray on social media?

Yeah. Not quite.

The first trimester, I had something – that, thanks to Kate Middleton, the world is more aware of – called Hyperemesis Gravidarum. It's a sexy name for 'extreme morning sickness', and whoever called it 'morning sickness' is a sick joker. I was sick all day! I was throwing up ten to fifteen times a day and I couldn't keep anything down, not even water. I ended up in hospital, sleeping most of the time (because if I was awake, I'd vomit), and just hoping this wouldn't go beyond the first trimester. My heart, love, and every fibre of respect in my body goes out to other HG mothers who have had to go through this.

Mine luckily subsided at week seventeen or eighteen, after many weeks of horror.

Enter: fibroids.

During my scan at twenty weeks, the obstetrician asked me 'do you know you have fibroids? I found two … oh …three … oh there is another one, four! It's like finding Easter eggs!'

If it got worse: morphine. Insert the shocked emoji face here!

When you have fibroids while you're pregnant, there's nothing they can do for you medically except for pain management. As the baby grew, the fibroids shrunk (as they didn't have access to enough nutrients), and this process was very painful and scarring – emotionally and physically.

In autumn 2023 – almost exactly a year after the wedding – Ben was born.

2024

Considering how hard the pregnancy was and all the complications that came with it, I decided to take a step back from my career.

I decided that I wanted to be present for Ben. I wanted to raise him. Like, *full time* raise him. I stayed home most of the time, doing admin for the business from home. When I did go to work in the kitchen, I took Ben with me. Which meant that my time in the kitchen was limited: I had to rush whatever I was doing so I could get Ben home for meals and nap time. I knew my work was not at its best. I put an ice to finishing this book, which is why it's taken four years to finish. Any projects that were not pressing, could wait.

I had one chance to raise this kid, and I wanted to give it my all.

But something else was on its way: in early 2024, I missed a call, and it went to my voicemail. That call was from the executive producer of MasterChef Australia. He gleefully asked me if I would consider competing in Australia Dessert Masters 2024, which would be filmed in April that year.

I remember hearing that voicemail and looking at Luke. I told him, 'They must be kidding! I literally haven't set foot in a kitchen for more than twelve months!' I couldn't remember the last time I made *macarons* or *choux* pastry; competing

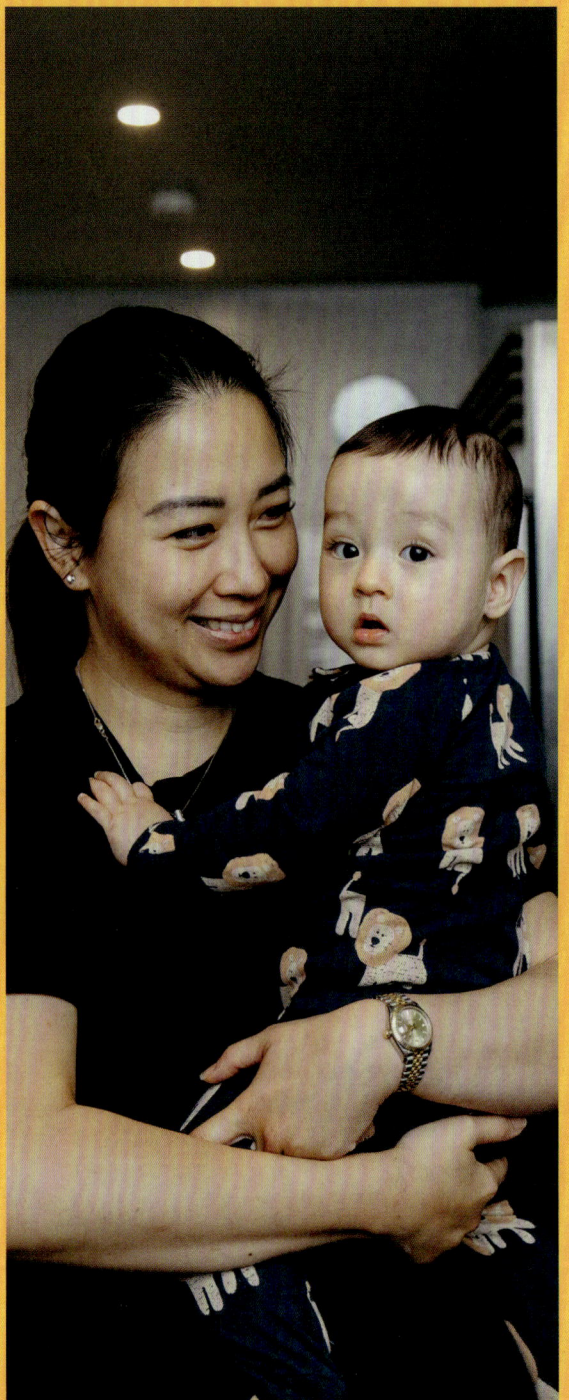

with some of the biggest names in the pastry world seemed out of the question. Competing in front of Amaury Guichon (someone I respect so much) and Melissa Leong (a fellow Asian woman in the culinary world and someone who I have lived through vicariously) felt impossible.

Luke just told me, 'Do it'.

This is one thing I love about him; that he has faith in me, much more than I have faith in myself. Every mother out there knows the meaning of 'self-doubt' *way* too well.

Luke told me that I shouldn't worry about going far, and to just have fun. He told me that I have what it takes, just like everyone else in that competition, to go as far as the end. He told me that not being in the kitchen for so long could be good for this, that I am not bound by technical aspects or trends that confine those who work in kitchens every day.

I took his advice and called the producer back.

What happened next is something for you to see unfold before your very own eyes. It's what I'm trying to communicate in this book: that if you master the basics – like Daniel-San in Karate Kid, wax-on and wax-off – your muscle memory will allow your imagination to soar, and you'll surprise even yourself!

Being a mother has taught me that even though you can imagine the world, what the world has in store for you is beyond what you can imagine; that the phrase 'your imagination is the limit' bears no validity.

There is *no limit*.

So please, keep on pushing, keep on practicing, keep on working on yourself. Because when your imagination becomes reality, you want to be ready for it.

120

advanced recipes

Running with Your Imagination
Advanced Recipes

So: you're ready to start using your imagination!

I always begin my creation from a sketch; a direct translation from what I imagine in my head. That sketch is then transformed into a final product, many steps and dances later, all made from basic recipes.

Once you master your basics, you will understand how each recipe works structurally, both alone and with other recipes. If mastering basic recipes is just like mastering your music chords, then this section is a lesson in architecture. You can make a cake look like a lot of things; I'm pretty sure you know that by now from so many viral videos of cakes that don't look like cakes! However, when you want that cake or dessert to have the complexity of multiple textures – from crunchy, spongey, airy and bite-y – you need to understand the structural integrity of your building blocks.

This process requires you to sketch and to refer to your basic recipe master list. It requires you to ask questions such as, 'Will this hold up the way I want it to?' and, 'Willl this cut easily? What experience will it give me when I dig in?'.

This section peels back those layers of creating a bespoke dessert, when a cake is more than just a cake – when dessert is not just dessert, but art.

123

Chocolate Tempering

I am going to try not to scare you with this chapter. However, if you want to create decorations for your desserts that are actually, well, nice to eat, you should be looking at using tempered chocolate rather than fondant, sugar, or other edible materials.

Instead of telling you why we must temper when we are working with chocolate, I'm just going to let you know what would happen if you didn't and went straight on to using untempered chocolate in your designs:

- Your chocolate would melt, super easily. This makes it harder for you to handle and work with, and impossible to unmould. Even if you put it in the coldest part of your fridge, it would just wilt and flop.

- Your chocolate would not have that wonderfully shiny surface (into which you can stare lovingly and ask 'who's the prettiest of them all').

- Your chocolate would taste strange and have a grainy, brittle texture.

In all honesty, chocolate tempering is not that hard, if you follow these rules strictly:

- Get a reliable digital thermometer. This is a must. The old-school way of touching it to your bottom lip to gauge the temperature is like saying you don't need an electric mixer and can beat everything by hand. We are in 2025! Get that digital thermometer!

- Don't let it touch water. Chocolate is like a gremlin. It does not like water of any kind: droplets, mists, humidity … all forbidden. The old method of Bain-Marie is not good for this reason. Melt it in the microwave instead.

- Make sure you have good chocolate *couvertures*. There are lots of great chocolate brands: Callebaut, Cocoa Barry, Weiss, and Valrhona for example. These brands, along with their variations, would most definitely have the tempering temperature instructions on their packaging. These packets also often have storage instructions; but usually, if you keep your chocolate below 25°C and in dark, dry environments, it'll be fine, so keep it in your pantry.

That's all basically. Not that complicated right?

Now, I am going to show you an example of a tempering temperature graph for *couverture*. Again, don't be scared, I will explain!

chocolate temperature curves (cont'd)

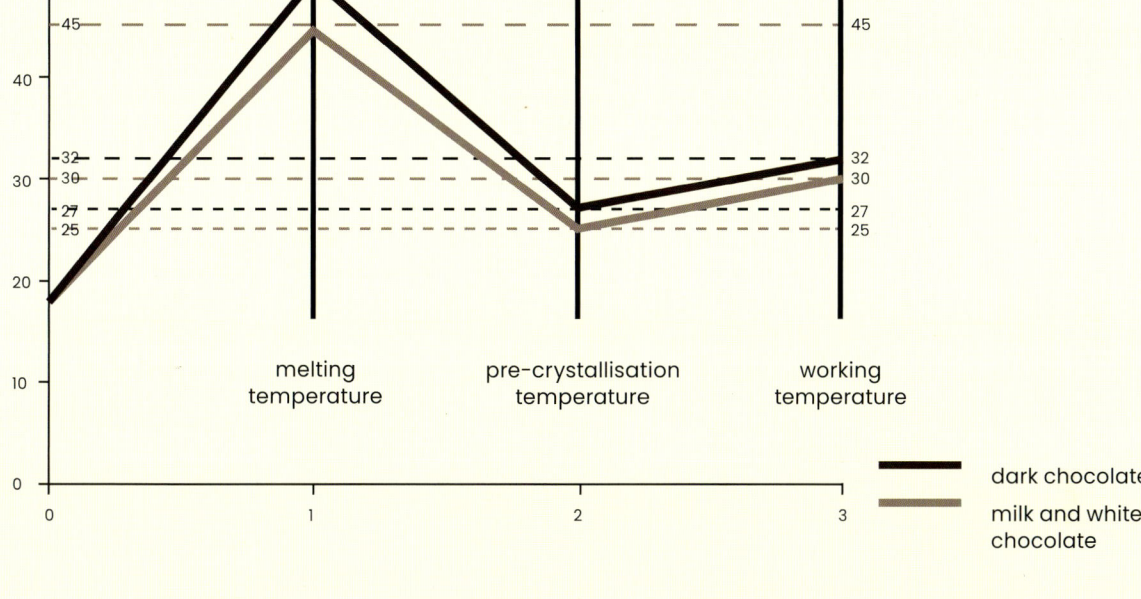

dark chocolate
milk and white chocolate

Every chocolate *couverture* has a different tempering temperature; this is just an example for a specific chocolate. Always check the packaging of your *couverture* for the recommended tempering temperature.

Now, chocolate has 3 different tempering temperatures:

1   Melting temperatures. The heat you need to achieve to properly melt it into a liquid. Don't go hotter than this, or you'll burn the chocolate.

2   Pre-crystallisation temperatures. This is the heat at which the crystal particles start to re-arrange themselves and create strong bonds that give the chocolate a sturdy and snappy texture.

3   Working temperatures (usually 2–3 degrees higher than the previous stage) at which your chocolate is perfect to work with.

So, you 'technically' have to bring the chocolate to 3 different temperatures to temper it. This is the textbook way, okay? This is the proper way. Please don't tell people I'm teaching you otherwise.

But …

All *couverture* chocolate, stored in the right environment and at the right temperature, comes fully tempered already. So, there is a quicker way to temper it, and that is to skip cooling it down to pre-crystallisation temperature and to go straight to the working temperature.

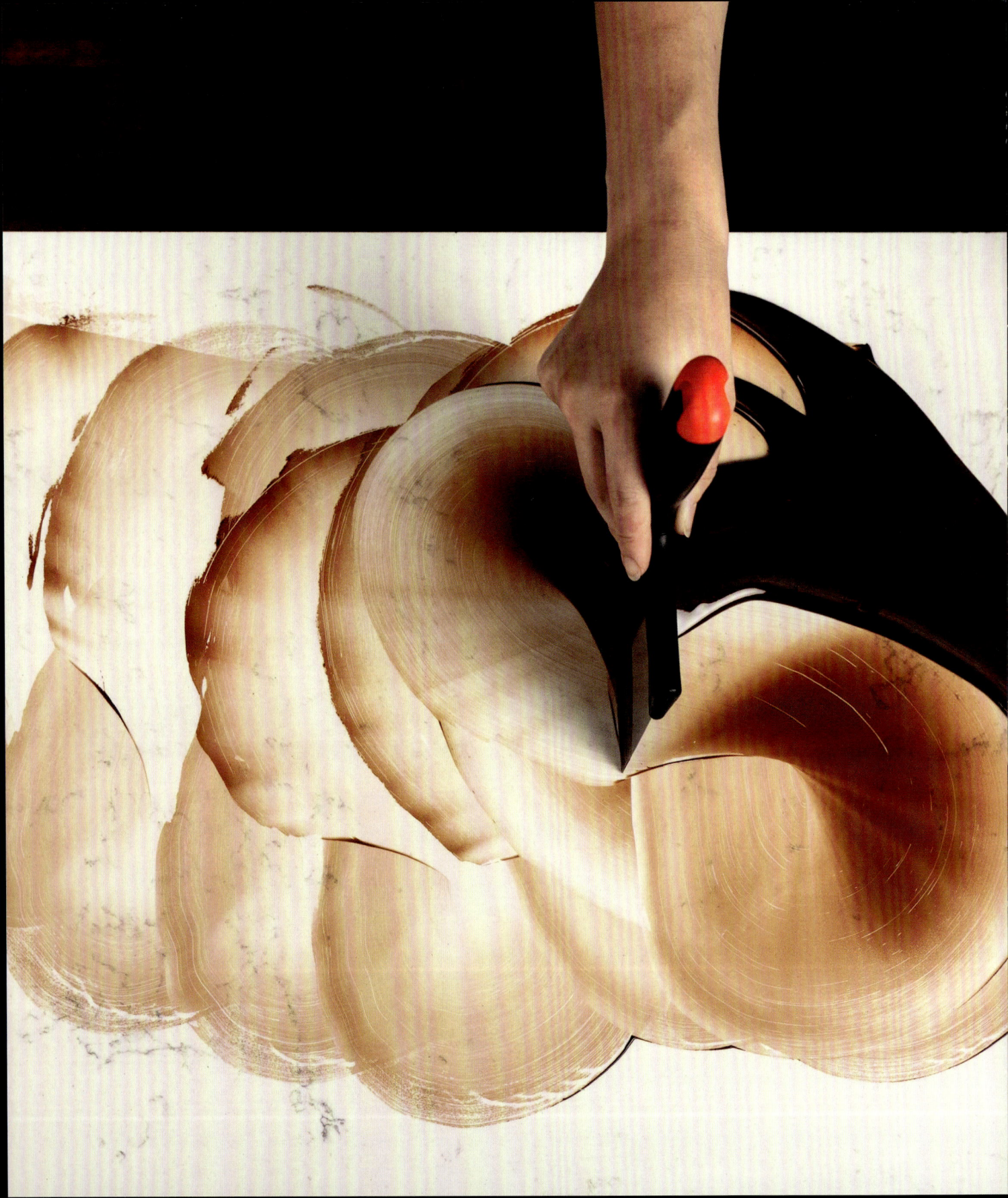

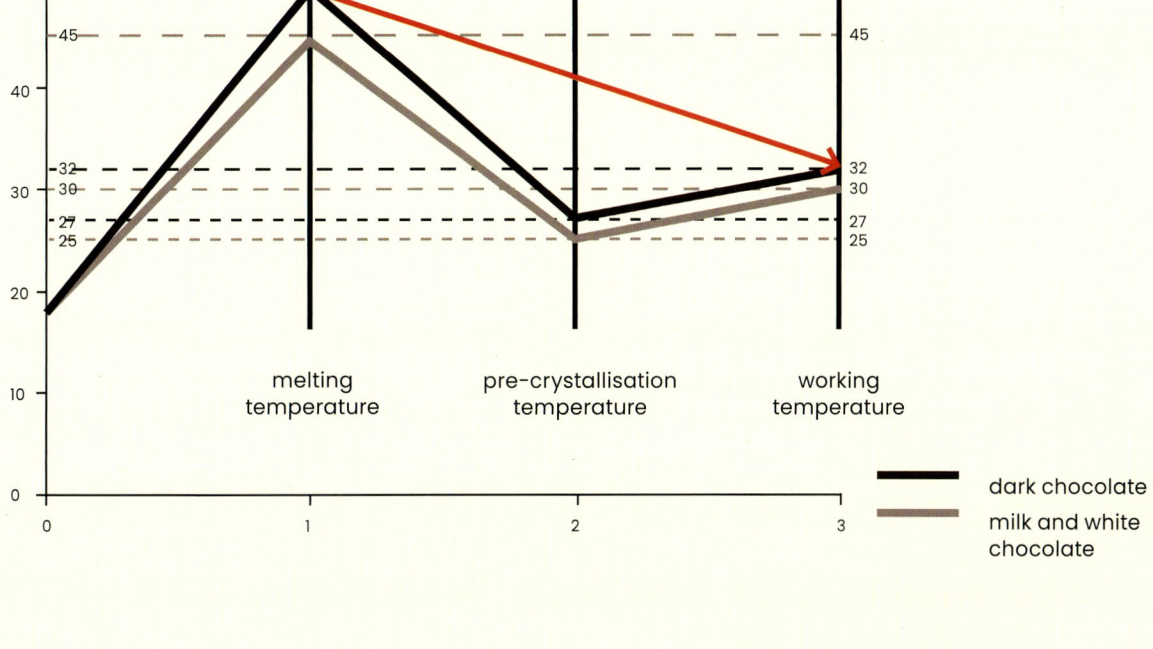

1. Grab your microwave-safe bowl. Place in ⅔ of the chocolate you want to temper into the bowl.

2. Melt it in 45-second blasts. This depends on how strong your microwave is, how much you are melting, and what you are melting (white chocolate melts quickest, and dark chocolate melts slowest). The higher the percentage of the cocoa mass, the sturdier the chocolate is and the longer you can stretch the blast.

3. Once everything is melted to the melting temperature (use the digital thermometer), put in the other ⅓ of the chocolate you want to melt and mix it with your melted chocolate. This will bring the temperature down quickly while melting the rest of the *couverture*. Give it a good stir and scrape on the sides every few minutes or so until it reaches working temperature.

And there you have it! The 101 of chocolate tempering. Make sure you follow the rules, buy decent quality chocolate *couvertures*, have a good digital thermometer, and you have won half of your battles.

Happy tempering!

Raspberry Mushroom

I got my first Head Chef opportunity in 2013, opening for Adelphi Hotel and Om Nom Dessert Bar. I created a dish that was inspired by the flavour of 'Ispahan' by Pierre Hermé, which is a combination of lychee, raspberry and rosewater.

Fast forward to now, and I have created so many different versions of this dish. It took me many, many, many trials to get to this version of the Raspberry Mushroom, which is now one of GLACÉ's signature cakes. This dessert really is the amalgamation of my journey.

Note: the given quantities will produce approximately 10–12 mushrooms.

134

advanced recipes

Raspberry *Ganache*

250	*Thickened Cream (A)*
180	*Frozen Raspberries*
150	*White Chocolate*
250	*Thickened Cream (B)*

1 *Sheet of Gelatine Leaves*

Method

1. Pre-soak gelatine in ice water. Once bloomed, squeeze to drain excess water. Place in a bowl with the white chocolate.

2. Heat thickened cream (A), vanilla and frozen raspberries in a saucepan on medium heat. Mix continuously with a rubber spatula until the mixture reaches 80°C.

3. Pour hot mixture over soaked gelatine and white chocolate, then blend with a hand blender until smooth and glossy.

4. Add thickened cream (B) and hand blend to combine.

5. Cover with cling film, pressing down so that the cling film is touching the surface of the mixture. Refrigerate overnight.

6. Once set, whip to soft peaks with a hand mixer, put in piping bag and set aside.

Lychee Jelly

260	*Lychee Purée*
55	*Sugar*
30	*Glucose*

2 *Sheets of Gelatine Leaves*

Method

1. Pre-soak gelatine in ice water. Once bloomed, squeeze to drain excess water.

2. Heat sugar, glucose and lychee *purée* in a saucepan on medium heat. Mix continuously with a rubber spatula until the mixture reaches 80°C.

3. Pour hot mixture over soaked gelatine, and blend with a hand blender until smooth and glossy.

4. Pour mixture into 5 cm half-sphere moulds, and set in the freezer for 2 hours minimum (or overnight if possible). Unmould and store in the freezer until ready to use.

raspberry mushroom

Dipping Glaze (White)

500	*White Chocolate*
165	*Cocoa Butter*
38	*Vegetable Oil*
QS	*White Liposoluble Food Colouring*

Method

1. Melt cocoa butter in the microwave at high setting in 30-second bursts.

2. Partially melt white chocolate in the microwave at high setting in 30-second bursts.

3. Add melted cocoa butter and vegetable oil to the white chocolate. Mix with a hand mixer until everything is well incorporated.

4. Add a tiny amount of white liposoluble food colouring, and blend again with hand blender.

5. Set aside and keep warm inside the microwave with the door closed.

Red Shiny Glaze

114	*Milk*
232	*Pouring Cream*
230	*Sugar (A)*
80	*Glucose*
72	*Sugar (B)*
20	*Cornflour*
QS	*Red Hydrosoluble Food Colouring*
QS	*Gold Dust*

2 Sheets of Gelatine Leaves

Method

1. Pre-soak gelatine in ice water. Once bloomed, squeeze to drain excess water.

2. Heat milk, pouring cream, sugar and glucose in a saucepan on the stove at medium heat, mixing continuously with a rubber spatula. Bring to a boil, then remove from the heat.

3. In a separate small bowl, whisk sugar (B) and cornflour together to break the lumps. With a ladle, scoop some of the hot cream mixture into the cornflour and sugar mixture and mix with a whisk until well combined and smooth.

4. Whisk in cornflour slurry to hot cream mixture and bring the mixture back to a boil, mixing continuously with a rubber spatula.

5. Remove from heat and add bloomed gelatine. Mix with a hand blender until smooth.

6. Add red food colouring and gold dust to achieve desired colour.

7. Let mixture cool in the fridge with cling film pressed down to touch the surface of the mixture all over.

8. To use, heat up glaze in the microwave to 26°C. Then, use a hand blender to blend until smooth and even in temperature throughout.

raspberry mushroom

To Assemble the Mushroom Cap

1. Pipe whipped raspberry *ganache* into 7 cm half-sphere moulds, filling each mould halfway to the top.

2. Place the frozen lychee jelly half-sphere into the centre of the raspberry *ganache*, then pipe more whipped *ganache* to cover the mould entirely. Use a small palette knife to scrape off excess whipped *ganache* and create a flat surface.

3. Freeze until solid and unmould.

4. Store in the freezer until ready to use.

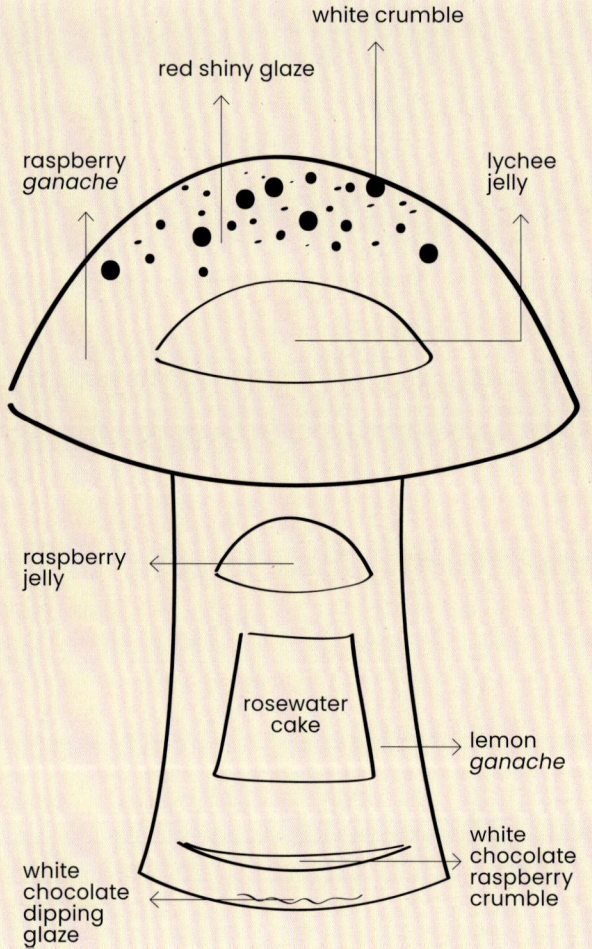

141

raspberry mushroom

Lemon *Ganache*

300	*Thickened Cream (A)*
100	*Lemon Purée*
QS	*Vanilla*
160	*White Chocolate*
300	*Thickened Cream (B)*

1 *Sheet of Gelatine Leaves*

Method

1. Pre-soak gelatine in ice water. Once bloomed, squeeze to drain excess water. Place in a bowl with the white chocolate.

2. Heat thickened cream (A), vanilla and lemon *purée* in a saucepan on medium heat. Mix continuously with a rubber spatula until the mixture reaches 80°C.

3. Pour hot mixture over soaked gelatine and white chocolate, then blend with a hand blender until smooth and glossy.

4. Add thickened cream (B) and hand blend to combine.

5. Cover with cling film, pressing down so that the cling film is touching the surface of the mixture. Refrigerate overnight.

6. Once set, whip to soft peaks with a hand mixer, put in piping bag and set aside.

Raspberry Jelly

100	*Frozen Raspberries*
250	*Raspberry Purée*
40	*Sugar*
30	*Glucose*

2 *Sheets of Gelatine Leaves*

Method

1. Pre-soak gelatine in ice water. Once bloomed, squeeze to drain excess water.

2. Heat sugar, glucose, raspberry *purée* and frozen raspberries in a saucepan on medium heat. Mix continuously with a rubber spatula until the mixture reaches 80°C.

3. Pour hot mixture over soaked gelatine, and blend with a hand blender until smooth and glossy.

4. Pour into 3 cm half-sphere moulds and set in freezer for 2 hours minimum (or overnight if possible). Unmould and store in the freezer until ready to use.

Raspberry Rosewater Cake

200	Eggs
140	Sugar
70	Brown Sugar
200	Plain Flour
10	Baking Powder
180	Butter (melted)
3	Salt
100	Frozen Raspberries (crushed)
50	Rosewater

Method

1. Preheat oven to 160°C (fan forced).
2. Mix all dry ingredients together in a mixing bowl and combine well. Set aside.
3. In a stand mixer bowl, use a whisk attachment to whip eggs and sugars on high speed until pale and fluffy. Scrape into large mixing bowl.
4. Add ⅓ of the dry ingredients into the whipped egg and sugar mixture, folding to combine with a rubber spatula.
5. Repeat until all dry ingredients are incorporated into the egg and sugar mixture, ⅓ at a time.
6. In a separate bowl, combine melted butter and salt.
7. Using a spoon, take out a small piece of batter and whisk into melted butter and salt until well combined. Then, fold this batter back through the big batch using a rubber spatula until well incorporated.
8. Fold in crushed frozen raspberries and rosewater.
9. Pipe into small *dariole* silicone moulds and bake for 13 minutes.
10. Leave to cool completely, then unmould and store in the freezer until ready to use.

Crumble

100	Butter (softened)
100	Plain Flour
100	Almond Meal
50	Sugar
50	Brown Sugar
3	Salt
2	Cinnamon Powder

Method

1 Preheat oven to 160°C (fan forced).

2 In a stand mixer bowl, use a paddle attachment to mix all ingredients until well incorporated and a pliable dough is formed.

3 Line a tray with baking paper. Place a wire rack on top of the tray and press dough through the wire rack to create even pieces. Remove the rack and distribute dough pieces evenly on the tray.

4 Place tray in oven for 15 minutes. Then, take tray out and use a metal scraper to scrape the pieces and roughly chop on tray.

5 Return the tray to the oven and bake for a further 15 minutes until pieces are golden brown in colour. If they're still pale, bake for another 5–10 minutes.

6 Cool crumble completely at room temperature before using.

Tip: For white crumble on top of the mushroom, mix some cooled crumble with titanium dioxide or white food colouring.

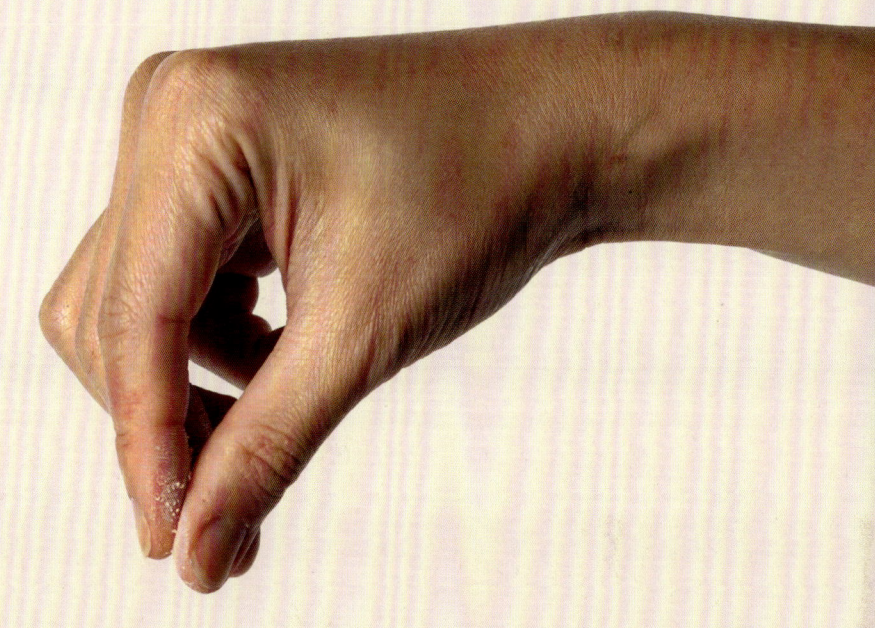

raspberry mushroom

Crunchy Raspberry Base

75	*White Chocolate*
60	*Butter (melted)*
2	*Salt*
200	*Crumble*
10	*Frozen Raspberries (crushed)*

Method

1. Preheat oven to 150°C (fan forced).

2. Place white chocolate on a silicone mat, or a tray lined with baking paper, making sure the blocks are dispersed evenly and flat on the tray.

3. Caramelise by baking in the oven for 15 minutes, turning the tray once in the middle of baking.

4. Once all white chocolate has melted and turned golden in colour, remove from the oven. Use a rubber spatula to carefully scrape the caramelised white chocolate into a mixing bowl.

5. Mix chocolate with melted butter and salt.

6. In a stand mixer bowl, add the caramelised white chocolate mixture to crumble and frozen raspberries. Use a paddle attachment to mix well until all ingredients are well incorporated.

7. Place mixture between sheets of baking paper or silicon mats, and roll out with a rolling pin to approximately 0.3 cm thickness. Place everything (including the baking papers or silicon mats) on a tray and freeze until stiff.

8. Using a 5 cm round cutter, cut the crunchy base into discs. Store discs in the freezer until ready to use.

To Assemble the Mushroom Stalk

1. Pipe whipped lemon *ganache* into dariole silicon moulds, filling them halfway up.
2. Press frozen raspberry jelly half-spheres into the middle part, followed by the rosewater cake. Pipe more whipped *ganache* to cover entirely.
3. Place crunchy raspberry base on top and press. Using small palette knife, scrape the excess whipped *ganache* to create flat surface.
4. Freeze until solid and unmould.
5. Store in the freezer until ready to use.

To Assemble the Mushroom

1. Warm a clean flat tray in the oven.
2. Run the flat bottom of the mushroom cap on the warm tray to gently melt the surface. Place this atop the smaller side of the still-frozen mushroom stalk.
3. Place your mushroom back in the freezer for 15 minutes.
4. Stick a skewer into the head of the mushroom and dip the entirety of the mushroom into the white dipping chocolate.
5. Before the chocolate sets, use a stiff brush to brush the base of the stalk in upwards motions.
6. Once the dipping chocolate hardens, blot some of the base of the stalk with cocoa powder using a dry soft brush.
7. Using your hand, hold the base of the stalk and dip the mushroom cap in the red shiny glaze. Lift up and allow some excess glaze to drip off.
8. Sprinkle some white crumble on top of your mushroom cap.

Rat! A Touille!

This rat was never meant to be one of our signature dishes. I created it for Lunar New Year 2020. Yeah, the year that the whole world went into lockdown from a little thing called COVID. The thing is, the rat sold really *really* well; people were even asking for it to be available during lockdown so they could buy it and drop it off to their loved ones to bring smiles to their faces. This was such a sweet notion to me. Also, *Ratatouille* is like, Luke's favourite Pixar movie.

Even if you look carefully, can you believe that this cute little thing basically comes from an egg mould? The power of imagination!

Note: the given quantities will produce approximately 10–12 rats.

Vanilla *Pannacotta*

250	*Milk*
100	*Pouring Cream*
80	*White Chocolate*
QS	*Vanilla*

2 Sheets of Gelatine Leaves

Method

1. Pre-soak gelatine in ice water. Once bloomed, squeeze to drain excess water. Place in a bowl with white chocolate.

2. Heat milk, pouring cream and vanilla in a saucepan on stove at medium heat to 80°C, mixing continuously with a rubber spatula.

3. Pour hot mixture over soaked gelatine and white chocolate, then blend with a hand blender until smooth and glossy.

4. Pour into 5 cm half-sphere moulds and set in the freezer for 2 hours minimum (or overnight if possible). Unmould and store in the freezer until ready to use.

Passionfruit *Crémeux*

250	Passionfruit Purée
230	Egg Yolks
120	Sugar
30	Potato Starch
250	Butter (cubed)

Method

1. Heat passionfruit *purée* in a saucepan on the stove at medium heat. Don't let it boil.

2. At the same time, in a separate bowl, use a hand whisk to beat egg yolks, sugar and potato starch vigorously until well combined.

3. Once *purée* is simmering, take off the heat and pour half into the egg yolks, sugar and starch mixture. Whisk with hand whisk until well incorporated.

4. Pour this mixture back into the saucepan with the other half of the liquid, and place back on the heat. Mix continuously using a rubber spatula, until the mixture reaches 85°C. Then remove from the heat.

5. Pour into a cooled mixing bowl to bring the temperature down quickly.

6. Add cubed butter to warm mixture and blend with hand blender until mixture is silky and smooth.

7. Pour mixture into 5 cm half-sphere moulds and freeze for 2–3 hours minimum (or overnight if possible). Unmould and store in the freezer until ready to use.

Dark Chocolate Almond Crumble

125	*Butter*
125	*Plain Flour*
125	*Almond Meal*
63	*Sugar*
63	*Brown Sugar*
4	*Salt*
4	*Cinnamon Powder*
125	*Dark Chocolate*

Method

1. Preheat oven to 160°C (fan forced).

2. In a stand mixer bowl, use a paddle attachment to mix all ingredients until well incorporated and a pliable dough is formed.

3. Line a tray with a silicon mat. Place a wire rack on top of the tray and press dough through the wire rack to create even pieces. Remove the rack and distribute dough pieces evenly on the tray.

4. Place tray in the oven for 15 minutes. Then, take tray out and use a metal scraper to scrape the pieces and roughly chop on tray.

5. Return the tray to the oven and bake for a further 15 minutes until pieces are golden brown in colour. If they're still pale, bake for another 5–10 minutes.

6. Cool crumble completely at room temperature.

7. Once cooled, fold in melted dark chocolate using a spatula until all crumble pieces are well coated with the chocolate. Spread pieces on a tray and leave to cool further at room temperature.

Dark & Milk Chocolate *Mousse*

125	*Thickened Cream*
125	*Milk*
QS	*Vanilla*
65	*Sugar*
80	*Egg Yolks*
145	*Dark Chocolate (72%)*
355	*Milk Chocolate*
1100	*Thickened Cream (semi-whipped)*

1 *Sheet of Gelatine Leaves*

Method

1. Pre-soak gelatine in ice water. Once bloomed, squeeze to drain excess water. Place in a bowl together with dark and milk chocolate, then set aside at room temperature.

2. Heat thickened cream, milk and vanilla in a saucepan on the stove at medium heat.

3. At the same time, in a separate bowl use a hand whisk to beat egg yolks and sugar vigorously until well combined.

4. Bring the thickened cream, milk and vanilla mixture to a simmer (don't let it boil!), then take the mixture off the heat. Pour ½ into the egg yolks and sugar mixture and hand whisk until well incorporated. Pour this mixture back into the saucepan with the other ½ of the thickened cream, milk and vanilla mixture, and place back on the stove.

5. Mix continuously using a rubber spatula, until the mixture reaches 85°C. Then remove from the heat.

6. Immediately pour the hot mixture over the soaked gelatine and chocolate. Blend with a hand blender until smooth and glossy.

7. Pour into a cooled mixing bowl to bring the temperature down quickly. Then, put this in the fridge to bring the temperature down to 40°C.

8. Fold semi-whipped thickened cream through the mixture using a rubber spatula.

9. Place *mousse* in a piping bag and set aside.

To Assemble the Rat Body

1. Combine the half-spheres of vanilla *pannacotta* and passionfruit *crémeux* into a ball. The icy cold surface on both flat sides will stick to each other. If they're difficult to stick, rub the flat sides on a warm flat tray and then quickly stick them together.

2. Pipe the chocolate mousse into the egg mould, filling ¾ of the way. Push the ball insert into middle of the *mousse*.

3. Cover up the vanilla and passionfruit ball and fill the rest of the egg mould with chocolate *mousse*, leaving around 2 mm from the top of the mould (which is the flat bottom of the egg).

4. Sprinkle in as much crumble as possible to fill in the 2 mm gap. Use a palette knife to press the crumble into a flat surface.

5. Freeze until completely firm, then unmould and store in the freezer until ready to decorate and finish.

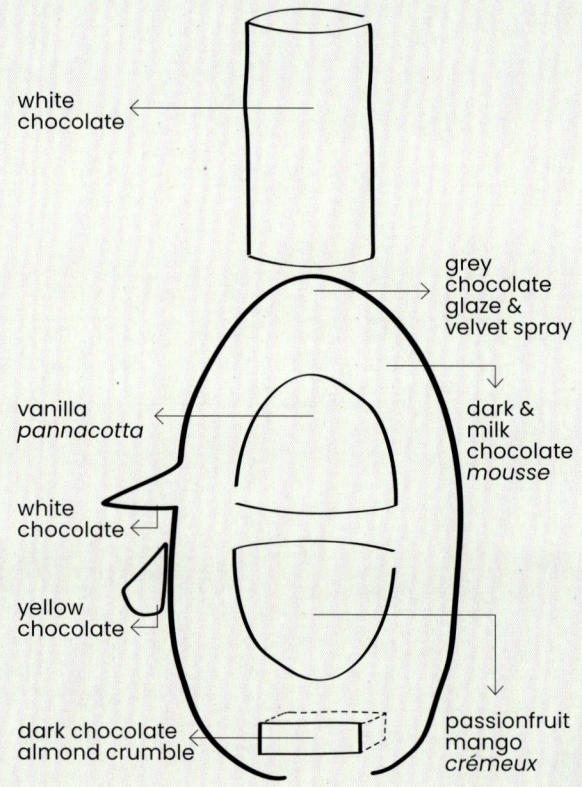

Dipping & Spraying Glaze (Grey)

500	*White Chocolate*
165	*Cocoa Butter*
38	*Vegetable Oil*
QS	*White Liposoluble Food Colouring*
QS	*Activated Charcoal Powder*

Method

1. Melt cocoa butter in microwave at high setting in 30-second bursts.

2. Semi-melt white chocolate in microwave at high setting in 30-second bursts. Add melted cocoa butter and vegetable oil. Use a hand blender to mix everything until well incorporated.

3. Add a tiny amount of white liposoluble food colouring and charcoal powder. Blend using a hand blender until desired grey colour is achieved.

4. Set aside and keep warm inside the microwave with the door closed.

157

rat! a touille!

advanced recipes

To Assemble the Rat

1. Place white chocolate buttons in a strong food processor and pulverise until a firm paste is formed. It should have a consistency similar to thick clay.

2. Place your hands in a tub of cold ice water, then dry completely. Take a small piece of the white chocolate clay and roll on a cool work bench into a small conical shape to form rat's nose. Set aside in the fridge until ready to use.

3. If the white chocolate clay firms up, blitz it again in the food processor to bring it back to its clay consistency.

4. Once done creating all the noses required, add yellow liposoluble food colouring to the white chocolate clay in the food processor and process further to create yellow chocolate clay.

5. Place your hands in a tub of cold ice water, then dry completely. Take a small piece of the yellow chocolate clay and roll on a cool work bench into a short, small cylinder to form a round block of 'cheese'. Using skewers, create different-sized holes in the cheese. Cut cheese into wedges. Set aside in the fridge 'till ready to use.

6. Cut clear acetate into 10 cm by 40 cm strips. Cut baking paper to the same size and quantity as acetate sheets. Wipe bench with damp cloth and lay acetate sheets on the damp bench to make them stick. Leave to let the damp bench dry completely.

7. Pour tempered white chocolate onto the acetate sheets. Use a palette knife to spread chocolate thinly and evenly into sheets of around 1 mm thickness. Wait until white chocolate crystallises (set, but not hard).

8. Using a clean knife and ruler, carefully cut strips of 8 cm width perpendicular to the 40 cm side, creating 5 rectangular strips of 10 cm by 8 cm. Cut gently to avoid slicing through the acetate.

9. Place a sheet of baking paper on top of the white chocolate and roll it around a 2 cm diameter pipe, starting on the 10 cm side. Tape the end of the acetate to keep it from unwrapping itself and let the chocolate crystallise further in the fridge for 10 minutes.

10. Once hardened, slide the pipe out. Carefully cut off the pieces of tape and use a toothpick to peel the acetate off the chocolate. You will now have 5 white chocolate cylinders, each 8 cm tall.

11. Repeat steps 6 to 10, but at step 6, cut 10 cm by 8 cm acetate strips, and at step 8 cut them into 10 cm by 2 cm chocolates. This will result in 5 white chocolate cylinders, each 2 cm tall.

12. Put a small knife into a cup of boiling hot water. Use the hot knife to make small slits – around 3-5 – on the top of the tall white chocolate cylinders.

13. Carefully stretch the short white chocolate cylinder, making it slightly wider. Gently slide the tall white cylinder through the inside of the shorter cylinder to create the base of the chef hat.

14. In a small piping bag, pour the remaining tempered white chocolate and pipe 2 solid circles of white chocolate onto baking paper or acetate to create the eyes.

15. In a small piping bag, pour in melted dark chocolate and dot the round white chocolates to create the pupils.

16. Take the frozen egg-shaped cakes out from the freezer and line them up on a tray. Take the noses out of the fridge. Leave to defrost a bit (around 5 minutes). Push the nose onto the egg and once all noses are attached, put the rats back in the freezer for 15–30 minutes.

17. Stick a skewer into the top part of the frozen egg-shaped cake, and dip the entirety of the egg into grey dipping glaze. Place it on a cool tray and quickly remove the skewer in a twisting motion. Leave it to rest in the freezer to keep it cold, but not for too long (30 minutes maximum).

18. Put the remaining grey glaze back into the microwave and warm it up. Pour this into the tank of a spray gun.

19. From about 30 cm away, spray the rats to create a fuzzy look.

20. Cool the leftover grey glaze until it thickens lightly and pour into small piping bag. Use this to attach the eyes and the wedges of cheese to the rats.

21. Melt some white chocolate and mix in red liposoluble colouring. Pour into a small piping bag and pipe it onto the tip of the rats' noses.

22. Run the base of chef hat on a warm tray and place it onto the head of the rat, pressing lightly so it sticks.

Tropic Thun-Bear

When we started GLACÉ back in 2017, it was supposed to be an ice cream shop. I was (and still am) obsessed by the art of making ice cream from what I saw in France. All the little cakes that were made of ice cream … just the sheer power and knowledge that is required for working with something so temperature-sensitive, so finicky, so delicate.

When we came out with a bear logo for the shop, it was only appropriate that we had a polar bear dessert, no? But I wanted it to be *polarising*. Polar bears live in cold climates, but this one brings warmth to your table, so I created it with tropical flavors; because I am also a tropical gal, and these flavors are my absolute jam.

Note: the given quantities will produce approximately 10–12 bears.

163

Coconut *Ganache*

125	*Thickened Cream (A)*
125	*Coconut Cream*
50	*White Chocolate*
125	*Thickened Cream (B)*

1 *Sheet of Gelatine Leaves*

Method

1. Pre-soak gelatine in ice water. Once bloomed, squeeze to drain excess water. Place in a bowl with the white chocolate.

2. Heat thickened cream (A), vanilla and coconut cream in a saucepan on medium heat. Mix continuously with a rubber spatula until the mixture reaches 80°C.

3. Pour hot mixture over soaked gelatine and white chocolate, then blend with a hand blender until smooth and glossy.

4. Add thickened cream (B) and a hand blend to combine.

5. Cover with cling film, pressing down so that the cling film is touching the surface of the mixture. Refrigerate overnight.

6. Once set, whip to soft peaks with hand mixer, put in piping bag, set aside.

Mango & Coconut Jelly

250	*Mango Purée*
63	*Passionfruit Purée*
63	*Coconut Cream*
75	*Glucose*
63	*Sugar*

4 *Sheets of Gelatine Leaves*

Method

1. Pre-soak gelatine in ice water. Once bloomed, squeeze to drain excess water.

2. Heat sugar, glucose, mango *purée*, passionfruit *purée* and coconut cream in a saucepan on medium heat. Mix continuously with a rubber spatula until the mixture reaches 80°C.

3. Pour hot mixture over soaked gelatine, and blend with a hand blender until smooth and glossy.

4. Pour mixture into 3 cm half-sphere moulds and set in freezer for 2 hours minimum (or overnight if possible). Unmould and store in the freezer until ready to use.

166

advanced recipes

To Assemble the Bear Head

1. Pipe whipped coconut *ganache* into 5 cm half-sphere moulds, filling them halfway up.
2. Place frozen mango and coconut jelly half-sphere into the middle, flat side up. Pipe more whipped *ganache* to cover the mould entirely. Use a small palette knife to scrape the excess whipped *ganache* to create flat surface.
3. Freeze to solid and unmould.
4. Warm a tray in the oven. Run the flat parts of 2 frozen 5 cm half-spheres on the warm tray to melt the surface a bit and then combine them, creating a full 5 cm round sphere.
5. Store in the freezer until ready to use.

Tropical *Crémeux*

90	Sugar
120	Passionfruit Purée
60	Frozen Banana
40	Lime Purée
QS	Eggs
300	Cold Butter (cubed)

1 *Sheet of Gelatine Leaves*

Method

1. Pre-soak gelatine in ice water. Once bloomed, squeeze to drain excess water.

2. Heat passionfruit *purée*, frozen banana, lime *purée* and vanilla in a saucepan on the stove at medium heat. Once liquid simmers (don't let it boil), take off the heat.

3. Use a hand blender to blend until smooth. Return to stove on medium heat.

4. At the same time, in a separate bowl, use a hand whisk to beat sugar and eggs vigorously until well combined.

5. Once liquid simmers (don't let it boil), take off the heat.

6. Pour half of the fruit mixture into the eggs and sugar mixture. Hand whisk until well incorporated. Pour this mixture back into the saucepan with the other half of the fruit mixture and place back on the stove, mixing continuously with a rubber spatula until it reaches 85°C. Then remove from the heat.

7. Pour hot mixture over soaked gelatine, then blend with hand blender until smooth and glossy.

8. Add the cold butter one cube at a time and continue blending with hand blender to cool, incorporate and emulsify everything.

9. Using piping bags, pipe *crémeux* into 5 cm half-sphere moulds and set in the freezer until solid.

10. Unmould and store in the freezer until ready to use.

Pineapple *Compote*

825	*Pineapple (peeled, brunoise)*
69	*Kalamansi Purée*
275	*Limee Purée*
172	*Mango Purée*
138	*Sugar*
QS	*Vanilla*

7 Sheets of Gelatine Leaves

Method

1. Pre-soak gelatine in ice water. Once bloomed, squeeze to drain excess water.

2. In a saucepan, caramelise sugar to a light/gold amber colour on the stove at medium heat.

3. Reduce heat and add the cubed pineapple, using the caramelised sugar as a glaze.

4. Add in lime *purée*, mango *purée* and kalamansi *purée*. Stir continuously with a rubber spatula.

5. Add vanilla, and cook for another 5 minutes.

6. Take mixure off the heat, then add gelatine. Mix well until all gelatine has dissolved. Then spread onto a tray.

7. Place in fridge to cool off.

8. Scoop the *compote* into 5 cm half-sphere moulds and place in the freezer. Once frozen, unmould and store in freezer until ready to use.

Coconut *Dacquoise*

215	*Egg Whites*
35	*Sugar*
180	*Icing Sugar (sieved)*
35	*Almond Meal*
140	*Desiccated Coconut*
QS	*Lime Zest*

Method

1. Preheat oven to 160°C (fan forced).

2. In a mixing bowl, use a whisk attachment to whisk egg whites and sugar at high speed until stiff peaks form.

3. In another bowl, combine all dry ingredients and lime zest. Use a rubber spatula to carefully fold in ½ of the stiff *meringue* until well incorporated. Then fold in the other ½ of the *meringue*.

4. Place mixture in a piping bag with a round nozzle.

5. Spray tray with a light oil and put baking paper on top (the oil is to stop the paper from moving around).

6. On the silicon mat, pipe mixture into circles of approximately 4–5 cm in diameter.

7. Bake the circles for 15 minutes. Take out of the oven and let them cool down completely before use.

To Assemble the Bear Body

1. Warm a tray in the oven. Run the flat part of frozen pineapple *compote* half-spheres and frozen tropical *crémeux* half-spheres on the tray, and then press them together to create full 5 cm sphere inserts.

2. Pipe whipped coconut *ganache* into 7 cm round sphere moulds, filling up halfway.

3. Place frozen round insert into the whipped *ganache*. Pipe more whipped *ganache* to cover ¾ of the mould.

4. Press in the coconut *dacquoise*, pipe more whipped *ganache* on top of it to cover the mould entirely. Use a small palette knife to scrape the excess whipped *ganache* to create flat surface.

5. Freeze to solid and unmould.

6. Store in the freezer until ready to use.

Dipping & Spraying Glaze (White)

215	*White Chocolate*
35	*Cocoa Butter*
180	*Vegetable Oil*
35	*Almond Meal*
QS	*White Liposoluble Food Colouring*

Method

1. Melt cocoa butter in the microwave at high setting in 30-second bursts.

2. Semi-melt white chocolate in the microwave at high setting in 30-second bursts. Add melted cocoa butter and vegetable oil. Use a hand blender to mix until everything is well incorporated.

3. Add a tiny amount of white liposoluble food colouring and blend again.

4. Set aside and keep warm inside the microwave with the door closed.

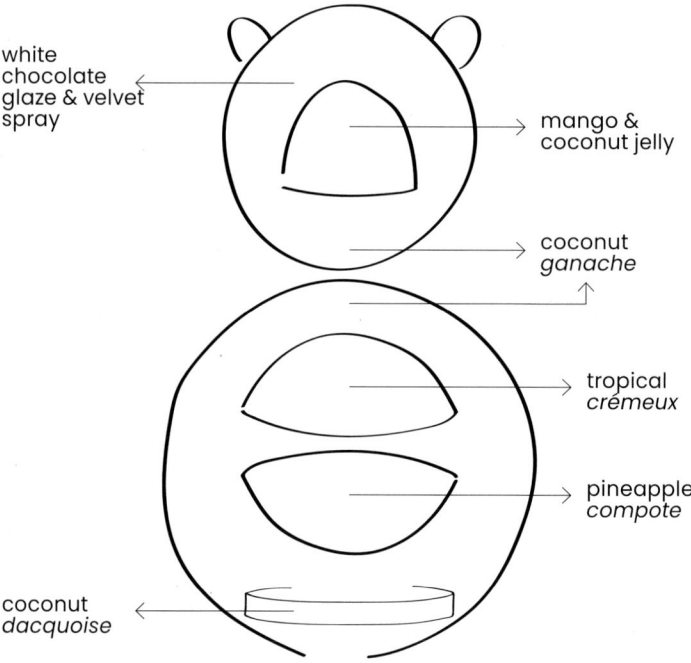

To Assemble the Bear

1. Warm a clean flat tray in the oven.

2. Run one side of the bear head part on the warm tray to gently flatten and lightly melt the surface.

3. At the same time, run the flat side of the bear body on the warm tray to gently flatten and lightly melt the surface.

4. Attach both parts together at the slightly melted surfaces.

5. Take a round white chocolate button (roughly 2 cm in diameter). Using the sharp part of a small heart cookie cutter, cut a small v shape out of the round button.

6. Gently press onto one side of the bear head. This will be the bear's muzzle.

7. Take 2 small white chocolate buttons (roughly 1 cm in diameter each) and gently press on to either side of the bear head. These will be the bear's ears.

8. Place bear back in the freezer for 30 minutes to let parts stick firmly to each other.

9. Stick a skewer into the head of the bear and dip the entirety of the bear into the white dipping chocolate. Place onto cold tray lined with baking paper and remove skewer with a twisting motion.

10. Put back in freezer to rest, for no longer than 30 minutes.

11. Warm the rest of the white glaze in the microwave. Pour into the tank of the spray gun through a small sieve.

12. Take bears out of the freezer, and from roughly 30 cm away spray the bear all over to create fuzzy look.

13. Melt some dark chocolate and place into a small piping bag.

14. Pipe a small heart shape at the tip of the bear's muzzle. Allow the chocolate to cool before serving.

Chocolate Excellence

Not everything here is 100% my pure creation. This one, which is actually my favourite to eat, belongs to Luke. He is very very *very* good at creating desserts that are so comforting and that you can eat again and again. Luke is a creature of routine. We both agree that, imagination wise, I probably have enough for the two of us. However, I can't sit still, and if I find a recipe that works perfectly, I can move on to create another new recipe. Why fix it if it's working and not broken, right?

Luke, on the other hand, is a quietly manic perfectionist. He had this cake made in so many different versions, in different shapes and sizes. This cake is a testament that sometimes, the most straightforward part of a dish – like the size of the moulds – can completely transform the eating experience.

Chocolate *Crémeux* (with egg)

265	*Milk*
135	*Pouring Cream*
QS	*Vanilla*
68	*Egg Yolks*
68	*Sugar*
225	*Dark Chocolate (58%)*

1 *Sheet of Gelatine Leaves*

Method

1. Pre-soak gelatine in ice water. Once bloomed, squeeze to drain excess water. Place in a bowl together with dark chocolate and set aside at room temperature.

2. Heat pouring cream, milk and vanilla in a saucepan on the stove at medium heat. Don't let this mixture boil.

3. At the same time, in a separate bowl, use a hand whisk to beat egg yolks and sugar vigorously until well combined.

4. Once the liquid in the saucepan is simmering, take off the heat and pour ½ into the egg yolks and sugar mixture. Whisk with hand whisk until well incorporated.

5. Pour this mixture back into the saucepan with the other ½ of the liquid, and place back on the heat. Mix continuously using a rubber spatula, until the mixture reaches 85°C. Then remove from the heat.

6. Pour the hot mixture over soaked gelatine and chocolate, then blend with a hand blender until smooth and glossy.

7. Pour mixture into a cooled mixing bowl (if you have a stainless steel one, place it in the freezer around 2 hours before cooking) to bring the temperature down quickly. Then, put this in the fridge to bring the temperature down further to 40°C.

8. Pour into a 7 cm disc mould or cake ring lined with acetate, creating a disc no taller than 1 cm.

9. Freeze until it reaches a solid state and then unmould.

Brownie

200	*Brown Sugar*
160	*Butter (softened)*
130	*Eggs*
90	*Dark Chocolate (58%) (melted)*
75	*Plain Flour*
7	*Cocoa Powder*
1	*Salt*

Method

1. Preheat oven to 160°C (fan forced).

2. In a stand mixer with a paddle attachment, add butter and brown sugar. At a medium-high speed, mix together until a pale and fluffy cream forms, stopping every few minutes or so to scrape the side with a rubber spatula.

3. Gradually add eggs and melted chocolate to butter mixture until well incorporated.

4. Reduce speed of mixer to medium, then sift in dry ingredients and continue mixing, stopping every few minutes or so to scrape the side until everything is mixed together.

5. Lightly spray baking tray with oil spray, and then line it with baking paper. Pour mixture into the tray.

6. Bake for 30 minutes. Once cooked, set aside to cool and flip it onto a tray. Peel off the baking paper and cut brownies into 7 cm discs using a round cutter.

Dark & Milk Chocolate *Mousse*

125	*Milk*
125	*Thickened Cream*
QS	*Vanilla*
65	*Sugar*
80	*Egg Yolks*
145	*Dark Chocolate (72%)*
355	*Milk Chocolate*
1100	*Cream (semi-whipped)*

1 *Sheet of Gelatine Leaves*

Method

1. Pre-soak gelatine in ice water. Once bloomed, squeeze to drain excess water. Place in a bowl together with dark and milk chocolate, then set aside at room temperature.

2. Heat thickened cream, milk and vanilla in a saucepan on the stove at medium heat.

3. At the same time, in a separate bowl use a hand whisk to beat egg yolks and sugar vigorously until well combined.

4. Bring the thickened cream, milk and vanilla mixture to a simmer (don't let it boil!), then take the mixture off the heat. Pour ½ into the egg yolks and sugar mixture and hand whisk until well incorporated. Pour this mixture back into the saucepan with the other ½ of the cream, milk and vanilla mixture, and place back on the stove.

5. Mix continuously using a rubber spatula, until the mixture reaches 85°C. Then remove from the heat.

6. Immediately pour the hot mixture over the soaked gelatine and chocolate. Blend with a hand blender until smooth and glossy.

7. Pour into a cooled mixing bowl to bring the temperature down quickly. Then, put this in the fridge to bring the temperature down further to 40°C.

8. Fold semi-whipped cream through the mixture using a rubber spatula.

Chocolate Shortcrust Pastry

235	*Plain Flour*
15	*Cocoa Powder*
94	*Icing Sugar*
31	*Almond Meal*
3	*Salt*
150	*Butter (chopped into small cubes)*
55	*Eggs*
QS	*Vanilla*

Method

1. Heat oven to 160°C (fan forced).

2. Combine all dry ingredients and butter in stand mixer bowl. Use a paddle attachment to mix at medium speed until mixture has a sandy consistency.

3. Still mixing, gradually add eggs and vanilla until a soft dough is formed.

4. Use a rolling pin to roll out pastry mixture between sheets of baking paper, creating pastry sheets of roughly 0.5 cm in thickness.

5. Leaving the pastry sheets between the sheets of baking paper, move pastry sheets onto the tray and freeze.

6. Once frozen, cut pastry into 8 cm discs using a round cutter. Store in the freezer until ready to use.

7. Arrange on a silicon mat and bake for 14 minutes. Leave to cool before using.

Dipping & Pouring Glaze (Rocher)

500	*Dark Chocolate (58%)*
165	*Cocoa Butter*
38	*Vegetable Oil*
150	*Whole Roasted Hazelnuts*

Method

1. Place roasted hazelnuts in a food processor and blitz in pulses to achieve a rough, chopped consistency.

2. In a microwave, melt chocolate, cocoa butter and vegetable oil together.

3. Fold chopped hazelnuts into the melted chocolate using a spatula.

To Assemble the Bottom Part

1. Put mousse into piping bag and pipe to fill ⅓ of pebble mould.

2. Add in the circle of dark chocolate brownie, and then pipe in more *mousse* on top to fill another ⅓ of pebble mould.

3. Put in the frozen *crémeux* disc and pipe in more *mousse* on top to fill the pebble mould completely. Use a small palette knife to spread the *mousse* to create a flat surface.

4. Freeze until solid and unmould. Store in the freezer if not using immediately.

5. Place some trays lined with silicon mats or baking paper in the freezer.

6. Insert a skewer into the top side of the pebble (*crémeux* side) and dip it into rocher glaze once to cover the side entirely, leaving the top part uncovered. Quickly place it on a cold tray to set.

7. Place chocolate shortcrust disc on the uncovered *mousse* side.

Hazelnut Base

50	*Butter (melted)*
100	*Milk Chocolate (melted)*
240	*Hazelnut Praliné*
80	*Crushed Hazelnut*
420	*Crumble*

Method

1. Melt butter and milk chocolate in a microwave in 20-second bursts.

2. Once completely melted, add hazelnut *praliné* and use a rubber spatula to mix until smooth.

3. Combine with crushed hazelnut and crumble.

4. Roll out mixture onto sheets of baking paper. Cover with another sheet of baking paper and use a rolling pin to roll mixture to chocolate sheets of roughly 0.5 cm thickness.

5. Still between the baking paper sheets, move chocolate onto a tray and freeze.

6. Once frozen, cut into 7 cm discs using a round cutter. Store in the freezer until ready to use.

Tip: To make your own hazelnut *praliné* paste, you will need equal amounts caramel and roasted hazelnuts. Pour the caramel over the hazelnuts and leave them to cool. Then, break the hazelnuts up into smaller pieces and blitz in a food processor until a smooth paste is formed.

Soft Salted Caramel

220	Sugar
220	Pouring Cream
4	Salt
QS	Vanilla
225	Butter (chopped)

Method

1. Warm cream, salt and vanilla in a saucepan on the stove at medium heat. Bring to a simmer then set aside.

2. In a separate saucepan on medium heat, sprinkle ⅓ of the sugar. Let it melt to caramelise to a light amber colour. Sprinkle another ⅓ of the sugar and use a rubber spatula to gently fold the sugar into the caramel to continue melting. Add the remaining ⅓ of the sugar and let it caramelise to a dark amber colour.

3. Reduce heat and deglaze the caramel with hot cream. Whisk to combine.

4. Once all combined, turn off the heat, add butter and continue whisking until smooth.

5. Cover with cling film, pressing down so it touches the mixture all over, and chill in the fridge overnight.

184

advanced recipes

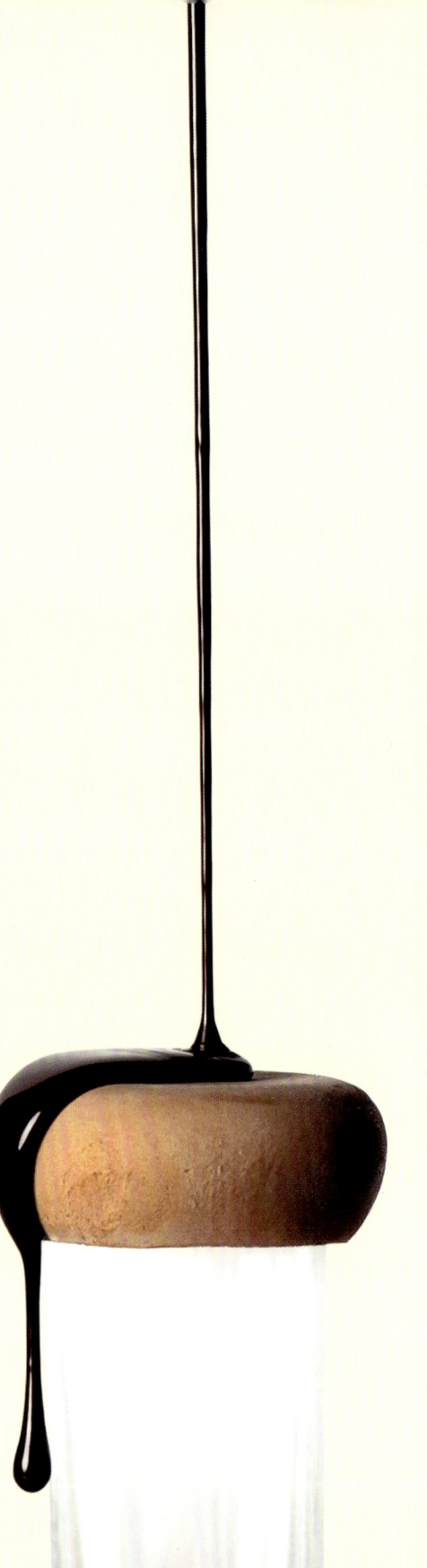

Dark Chocolate Shiny Glaze

130	*Water*
300	*Glucose Syrup*
300	*Sugar*
200	*Condensed Milk*
280	*Dark Chocolate (58%)*

3 *Sheets of Gelatine Leaves*

Method

1. Pre-soak gelatine in ice water. Once bloomed, drain excess water.

2. Heat water, glucose and sugar in a pot on the stove at medium heat, to 103°C.

3. Carefully pour hot mixture over the chocolate, condensed milk and bloomed gelatine. Mix with a hand blender until smooth and glossy.

4. Leave to rest in the fridge for 12 hours, with cling film pressed down so it is touching the surface all over.

5. When ready to use, heat up glaze in the microwave with 20-second bursts, mixing well in between using a spatula until temperature reaches 27°C.

To Assemble the Top Part

1. Put *mousse* into piping bag and pipe to fill ⅔ of pebble mould.

2. Using a small palette knife in an upward motion, spread the chocolate *mousse* around the inner side of the mould creating a well at the centre of the mould.

3. Put soft salted caramel into a piping bag and pipe some into the well.

4. Pipe in more *mousse* on top to fill the pebble mould completely. Using small palette knife, spread the *mousse* to create a flat surface.

5. Place the hazelnut crunchy base on top and push lightly onto the flat *mousse* surface to stick it on.

6. Freeze until solid and unmould. Store in the freezer if not using immediately.

7. Place a wire rack on a baking tray and put some frozen 'pebbles' on the wire rack, spaced evenly.

8. Pour shiny chocolate glaze over each. Slot a small palette knife under each glazed top part and move around slowly to shake the excess glaze off. Carefully place them on top of the assembled bottom part.

To Decorate

1. Spread tempered dark chocolate thinly on rectangle acetate sheets (roughly 30 cm by 40 cm in size). Sprinkle some chopped roasted hazelnut over the chocolate. Place another acetate sheet on top before letting the chocolate set.

2. Roll the sheets around a 2.5 cm pvc pipe, securing the end with tape.

3. Let tubes rest in the fridge for a minimum of 15 minutes.

4. Slide the pvc pipe out of the inside of the chocolate, leaving behind a chocolate tube wrapped in acetate sheets. Cut the tape off and peel the acetate sheet from the chocolate, letting the chocolate sheets naturally break off in curved shapes.

5. Place one shard on top of the dish and spray some gold dust to finish.

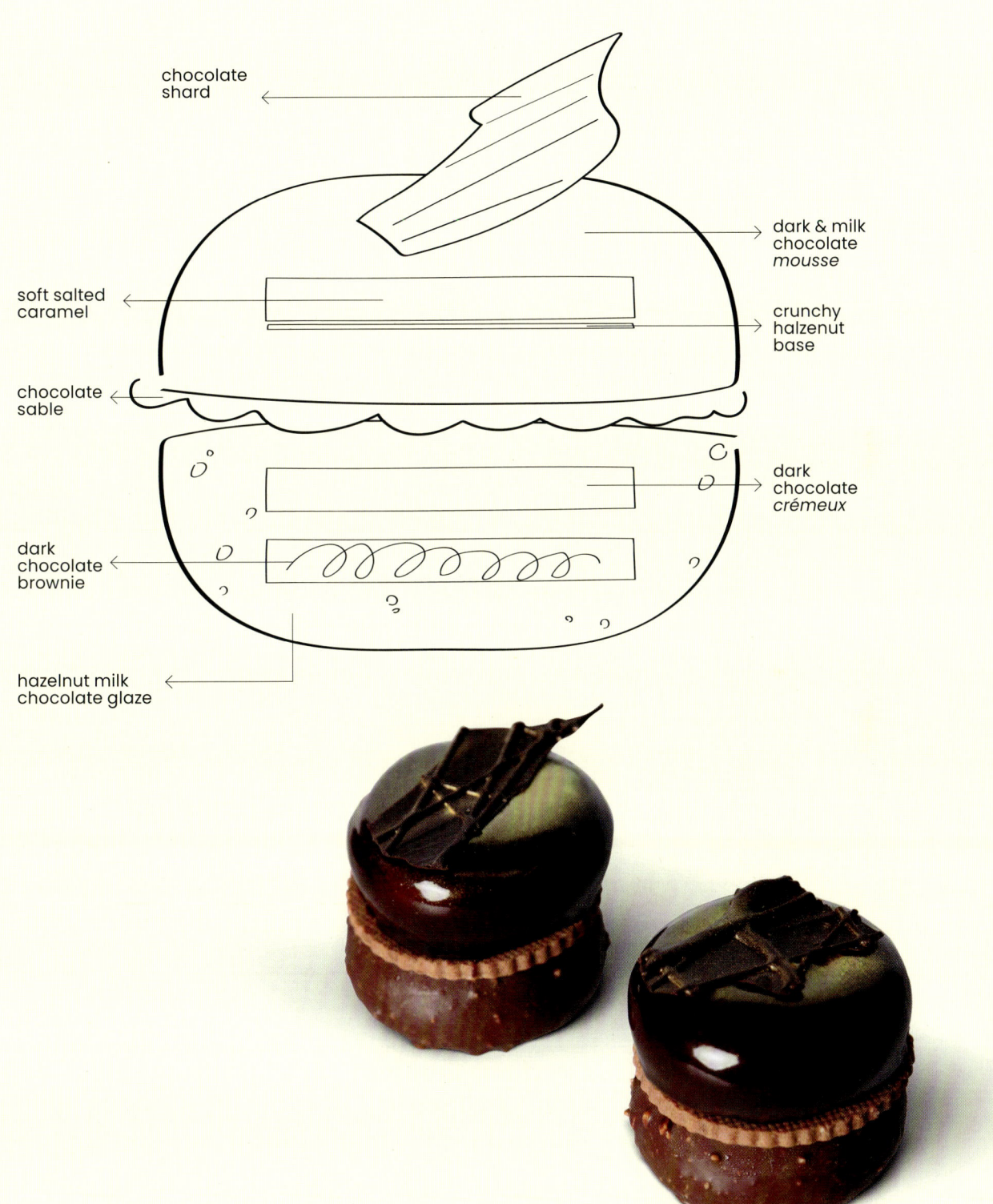

chocolate excellence

Rubik's Cube

When they announced on Dessert Masters that we were going to make a moving dish, my first thought was Ben's first birthday cake. I made that thing turn by using the motor from an old-school fishing toy. However, there was no such toy readily available in the Dessert Masters kitchen, was there?

So, I had to improvise. I had to make the moving part from whatever I could make that day. We had tanks of tempered chocolate there and I just decided to make the entire moving structure out of chocolate. Bold? Yes. Crazy? 3000%. Did it work? You bet it did.

Would I do it again in 2.5 hours? No thank you.

Tropical *Compote*

34	*Sugar (A)*
240	*Frozen Banana*
60	*Mango Purée*
40	*Passionfruit Purée*
20	*Glucose*
QS	*Vanilla*
35	*Sugar (B)*
5	*Pectine NH*
15	*Kalamansi Purée*

2 *Sheets of Gelatine Leaves*

Method

1. Pre-soak gelatine in ice water. Once bloomed, drain excess water.

2. Roast frozen banana on a silicon mat in the oven at 150°C for 20 minutes.

3. In a medium pot on the stove at medium heat, bring sugar (A), roasted banana, mango *purée*, passionfruit *purée* and glucose to boil, mixing continuously with a rubber spatula.

4. In a separate mixing bowl, whisk sugar (B) and pectin together with hand whisk to break any lumps and add to boiling *purée* mix. Bring mixture to 105°C while continuously mixing with a rubber spatula.

5. Remove from heat and add soaked gelatine and kalamansi *purée*. Using a hand blender, process until smooth. Set aside in a mixing bowl in the fridge, with plastic film pressed down to be touching the mixture all over, until cooled completely.

Coconut *Mousse*

375	Coconut Purée/Cream
30	Water
105	Sugar
56	Egg Whites
280	Thickened Cream (semi-whipped)

3 *Sheets of Gelatine Leaves*

Method

1. Pre-soak gelatine in ice water. Once bloomed, squeeze to drain excess water. Set aside at room temperature.

2. Heat coconut cream on the stove at medium heat. Bring this to a simmer (don't let it boil!), then add bloomed gelatine and whisk gently with hand whisk until all gelatine is dissolved. Set aside at room temperature.

3. Place egg whites in the bowl of a stand mixer. Use a whisk attachment and start mixing at low speed.

4. At the same time, place water and sugar in a saucepan and heat on stove at high heat. Place candy thermometer in the saucepan.

5. Once thermometer reads 110°C, increase the speed of the stand mixer to high.

6. Once thermometer reads 118°C, take saucepan off the heat and tap carefully on the bench to stop bubbles from forming.

7. Reduce the speed of the stand mixer to medium.

8. Once the saucepan syrup becomes clear, carefully pour it in a slow stream into the egg whites in the stand mixer (still whisking on medium). Be careful not to pour the hot sugar syrup onto the moving whisk: drizzle it between the moving whisk and the wall of the mixing bowl.

9. Once all hot sugar syrup is poured, increase the speed of the whisk to high and continue whisking until stiff *meringue* forms and the mixture cools to room temperature.

10. In a big mixing bowl, add ⅓ of the *meringue* and ½ of the warm coconut cream and gelatine mixture. Use a hand whisk to carefully fold them together.

11. Add another ⅓ of the *meringue* and the other ½ of the warm coconut cream and gelatine mixture. Continue whisking slowly.

12. Add the final ⅓ of the *meringue* and whisk until there are no *meringue* lumps present in the mixture.

13. Check the temperature of the mixture. Once it is under 40°C, fold in the whipped cream with a rubber spatula.

14. Use or pipe immediately, as the mixture will set once cold.

Dipping Glaze (White)

250	*White Chocolate*
250	*Cocoa Butter*

Method

Melt white chocolate and cocoa butter in the microwave using a microwave-safe bowl in 15-second intervals on high. Mix everything with a rubber spatula in between bursts. Once well melted, set aside at room temperature.

To Assemble the Tropical Cube

1. Pipe tropical *compote* into mini truffle moulds (approximately 2 cm in diameter).

2. Freeze until completely hard, then unmould and store in the freezer.

3. Pipe coconut *mousse* into cube moulds, filling about halfway.

4. Take the frozen tropical *compote* truffle and insert into the centre of the half-filled cube mould. Add more *mousse* if necessary and level the top of the cube. Freeze until completely hard.

5. Unmould the cube and, using a skewer or toothpick, prick one side of the frozen cube and dip into the white chocolate glaze.

Raspberry Jelly

110	*Frozen Raspberries*
250	*Raspberry Purée*
40	*Sugar*
30	*Glucose*

2 *Sheets of Gelatine Leaves*

Method

1. Pre-soak gelatine in ice water. Once bloomed, squeeze to drain excess water.

2. Heat sugar, glucose, raspberry *purée* and frozen raspberries in a saucepan on medium heat. Mix continuously with a rubber spatula until the mixture reaches 80°C.

3. Pour hot mixture over soaked gelatine, and blend with a hand blender until smooth and glossy.

4. Keep aside in the fridge, with cling film pressed down to touch the mixture all over, until completely cooled.

Pistachio Diplomat *Crème*

250	*Milk*
QS	*Vanilla*
60	*Sugar*
20	*Cornflour*
50	*Egg Yolks*
20	*Butter (chopped)*
70	*Pistachio Paste*
250	*Thickened Cream (semi-whipped)*

1 *Sheet of Gelatine Leaves*

Method

1. Pre-soak gelatine in ice water. Once bloomed, squeeze to drain excess water. Place in a bowl with the pistachio paste and cubed butter and set aside at room temperature.

2. Heat milk and vanilla in a saucepan on the stove at medium heat. Don't let this mixture boil.

3. At the same time, in a separate bowl, use a hand whisk to beat egg yolks, cornflour and sugar vigorously until well combined.

4. Once the liquid in the saucepan is simmering, take off the heat and pour half into the egg yolks, cornflour and sugar mixture. Whisk with hand whisk until well incorporated.

5. Pour this mixture back into the saucepan with the other half of the liquid, and place back on the heat. Mix continuously using a rubber spatula until the mixture reaches 85°C. Then remove from the heat.

6. Pour mixture over gelatine, pistachio paste and cubed butter, then blend with a hand blender until smooth and glossy.

7. Pour into a cooled mixing bowl to bring the temperature down quickly. Then, put this in the fridge to bring the temperature down further to 40°C.

8. Fold through semi-whipped thickened cream using a rubber spatula.

Dipping Glaze (Green)

250	*White Chocolate*
250	*Cocoa Butter*
QS	*Green Liposoluble Food Colouring*

Method

Melt white chocolate and cocoa butter in the microwave using a microwave-safe bowl in 15-second intervals on high. Mix everything with a rubber spatula in between bursts. Once well melted, add green food colouring and mix well with a hand blender. Set aside at room temperature.

Dipping Glaze (Red)

250	*White Chocolate*
250	*Cocoa Butter*
QS	*Red Liposoluble Food Colouring*

Method

Melt white chocolate and cocoa butter in the microwave using a microwave-safe bowl in 15-second intervals on high. Mix everything with a rubber spatula in between bursts. Once well melted, add red food colouring and mix well with a hand blender. Set aside at room temperature.

To Assemble the Pistachio Cube

1. Pipe raspberry jelly into mini truffle moulds (approximately 2 cm in diameter).

2. Freeze until completely hard, then unmould and store in the freezer.

3. Pipe pistachio *mousse* into cube moulds, filling about halfway.

4. Take the frozen raspberry jelly truffle and insert into the centre of the half-filled cube mould. Add more *mousse* if necessary and level the top of the cube. Freeze until completely hard.

5. Unmould the cube and, using a skewer or toothpick, prick one side of the frozen cube and dip into the red or green glaze.

199

rubik's cube

200

advanced recipes

Dark Chocolate *Mousse*

125	*Milk*
QS	*Vanilla*
30	*Sugar*
25	*Egg Yolks*
175	*Dark Chocolate (Cuvée Grand Cru 75%)*
385	*Thickened Cream (semi-whipped)*

1 *Sheet of Gelatine Leaves*

Method

1. Pre-soak gelatine in ice water. Once bloomed, squeeze to drain excess water. Place in a bowl together with dark chocolate, then set aside at room temperature.

2. Heat thickened cream, milk and vanilla in a saucepan on the stove at medium heat.

3. At the same time, in a separate bowl use a hand whisk to beat egg yolks and sugar vigorously until well combined.

4. Bring the thickened cream, milk and vanilla mixture to a simmer (don't let it boil!), then take mixture off the heat. Pour ½ into the egg yolks and sugar mixture and hand whisk until well incorporated. Pour this mixture back into the saucepan with the other ½ of the cream, milk and vanilla mixture, and place back on the stove top.

5. Mix continuously using a rubber spatula until the mixture reaches 85°C. Then remove from the heat.

6. Immediately pour the hot mixture over the soaked gelatine and chocolate. Blend with a hand blender until smooth and glossy.

7. Pour into a cooled mixing bowl to bring the temperature down quickly. Then, put this in the fridge to bring the temperature down to 40°C.

8. Fold semi-whipped thickened cream through the mixture using a rubber spatula.

Rum Salted Caramel

110	*Sugar*
110	*Pouring Cream*
3	*Salt*
QS	*Vanilla*
15	*Dark Rum*
110	*Butter (chopped)*

Method

1. In a small, deep stock pot on medium heat, add ½ the sugar and caramelise to a light amber colour. Then, sprinkle in the other ½ of the sugar and continue to caramelise until a dark amber colour. Don't agitate the sugar too much.

2. At the same time, in another small stock pot, warm pouring cream and vanilla to a simmer (not a boil).

3. Turn down the heat on the caramel and deglaze by carefully pouring hot cream mixture over it. Be careful of hot splatters!

4. Whisk with a hand whisk until well combned, then take off the heat.

5. Gradually add chopped butter while still whisking. Once all butter is melted and the mixture has cooled, add the rum (optional) and whisk again until well combined.

6. Cover with cling film, pressed down so it is touching the mixture all over, and chill in the fridge overnight.

Dipping Glaze (Dark Chocolate)

250	*Dark Chocolate*
250	*Cocoa Butter*

Method

Melt dark chocolate and cocoa butter in the microwave using a microwave-safe bowl in 15-second intervals on high. Mix everything with a rubber spatula in between bursts. Once well melted, set aside at room temperature.

To Assemble the Chocolate Cube

1. Pour tempered dark chocolate over 2.6 cm dome moulds, creating half-sphere shells of chocolate. Once hardened a bit, tip the shells over and scrape the edge surfaces so they're level. Put the shells in the fridge to crystalise.
2. Once the shells have crystalised, fill them with chopped roasted hazelnuts and crunchy chocolate pearls.
3. Pipe rum salted caramel over the hazelnuts and pearls, creating a flat surface level with the edge of the shell.
4. Place in freezer and leave the half-spheres to set until completely hard.
5. Pipe dark chocolate *mousse* into cube moulds, filling about halfway.
6. Take the frozen rum caramel inserts, and combine 2 together to make a ball.
7. Insert the rum and caramel ball into the centre of the half-filled cube mould. Add more *mousse* if necessary and level the top of the cube. Freeze until completely hard.
8. Unmould the cube and, using a skewer or toothpick, prick one side of the frozen cube and dip into the dark chocolate glaze.

To Assemble the Chocolate Structure

Other Ingredients

- Tempered Dark Chocolate
- Tempered White Chocolate
- Dark Chocolate Coated Crunchy Pearls (you can find these at most baking specialty stores)
- Roasted Hazelnut Piedmontese (skin off)
- Liposoluble Red Colouring
- Liposoluble Green Colouring

Other Equipment

- Silicone Mat Frame (tapis)
- Stainless Steel Ruler
- Round Circle Cutter
- Skewers Stick
- Chocolate Cold Spray
- Square 3.5 cm Moulds x4
- Mini Truffle Moulds x2
- 2.6 cm Dome Moulds x2
- Microplane Grater

Method

1. Pour tempered dark chocolate onto a silicon mat frame making sure it is level throughout. Put in fridge to semi set.

2. Once semi set, using a small knife cut 3 pieces of 12 cm by 12 cm squares and use the smallest round cutter to cut a circle out of the middle of each square (leave the round cut-outs in the chocolate frame). Put back in fridge to finish crystallising.

3. Pour tempered dark chocolate onto cube silicon mould. Fill 2 completely to the top, and 2 around 12 g full.

4. Freeze until completely hard. Then unmould all parts.

5. Follow assembly as below, attaching each part with tempered chocolate as glue.

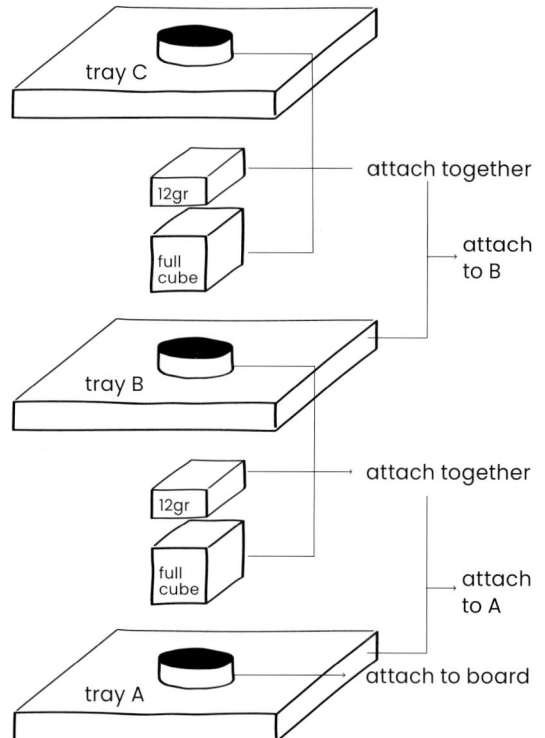

6. Place cubes, alternating colours, onto the structure. The first and second level comprise of 8 cubes, and the top level comprises of 9 cubes (as one goes in the centre).

"All Eyes On Me"

I have never been to a circus. No word of a lie. Well, okay, if you count the small tent traveling circus in a very tiny town in Yssingeux, France where I studied pastry as a 'circus' then I went to one. It only had a bunch of clowns smacking each others' heads. When I opened the Dessert Masters doors and in jumped some of Cirque de Soleil's performers, I was shook! Seeing them contorting and balancing – defying gravity – was so cool and exhilarating.

I know the circus supposedly brings childhood memories and this kind of nostalgic feeling. So, I decided to bring that into my dessert. Something so nostalgic and comforting but contrasting it with an exhilarating factor. I think it worked! Everyone held their breaths when I walked in with this contraption; me included.

Chocolate *Génoise*

240	*Egg Yolks*
210	*Sugar (A)*
240	*Egg Whites*
55	*Sugar*
110	*Plain Flour*
75	*Cocoa Butter*
75	*Butter (melted)*

Method

1. Pre-heat the oven to 175°C (fan forced).
2. Sift flour and cocoa powder together in a bowl. Set aside.
3. In a stand mixer bowl, use a whisk attachment to whip egg yolks and sugar (A) until pale, then transfer to a large mixing bowl.
4. In another stand mixer bowl, use a different or completely cleaned and dried whisk attachment to whip egg white and sugar (B) to stiff peaks and until the mixture doubles in volume (be careful not to over-whip).
5. Sift in ⅓ of dry ingredients into egg yolks mixture and carefully fold using a rubber spatula.
6. Fold in ⅓ of *meringue* and carefully fold using a rubber spatula.
7. Repeat steps 5 and 6 until all egg yolks mixture, *meringue* and dry ingredients are well incorporated together.
8. Carefully pour in melted butter and fold well using a rubber spatula.
9. Spread evenly onto a silicone mat frame. Bake for 14 minutes.
10. Take out of oven, and let it cool down completely.
11. Cut into 3 separate 12 cm diameter discs.

Chocolate *Crémeux* (with egg)

260	*Milk*
140	*Pouring Cream*
QS	*Vanilla*
70	*Egg Yolks*
70	*Sugar*
220	*Dark Chocolate (75%)*

1 *Sheet of Gelatine Leaves*

Method

1. Pre-soak gelatine in ice water. Once bloomed, squeeze to drain excess water. Place in a bowl together with dark chocolate and set aside at room temperature.

2. Heat pouring cream, milk and vanilla in a saucepan on the stove at medium heat. Don't let this mixture boil.

3. At the same time, in a separate bowl, use a hand whisk to beat egg yolks and sugar vigorously until well combined.

4. Once the liquid in the saucepan is simmering, take off the heat and pour ½ into the egg yolks and sugar mixture. Whisk with hand whisk until well incorporated.

5. Pour this mixture back into the saucepan with the other ½ of the liquid, and place back on the heat. Mix continuously using rubber spatula until the mixture reaches 85°C. Then remove from the heat.

6. Pour the hot mixture over soaked gelatine and chocolate, the blend with a hand blender until smooth and glossy.

7. Pour into a cooled mixing bowl to bring the temperature down quickly. Place it back in the fridge to cool it down further.

8. Pour about 1 cm of mixture into 7 cm cylinder moulds, and freeze.

Cherry Jam

100	*Guinettes Cherry (chopped)*
90	*Sour Cherry Purée*
QS	*Vanilla*
45	*Sugar*
2	*Pectin NH*

Method

1. In a small saucepan on medium heat, mix together guinettes cherry, sour cherry *purée*, vanilla and 30 g of sugar until boiling.

2. In a separate mixing bowl, use a hand whisk to mix 15 g of sugar with the pectin NH and whisk well to break up any lumps. Incorporate into the hot mixture once it reaches 100°C and continue mixing with a rubber spatula.

3. Bring the mixture up to 105°C.

4. Pour mixture into a cooled mixing bowl to bring the temperature down quickly. Place it back in the fridge to cool it down further.

5. Once cooled, place mixture into a piping bag.

Tip: *Guinettes* cherry is a type of cherry macerated in liquor. you can buy this in gourmet ingredients shops. They are a luxurious alternative to maraschino cherries, offering a more complex and refined taste.

211

"all eyes on me"

Vanilla *Mousse*

330	*Milk*
QS	*Vanilla*
60	*Sugar*
26	*Cornflour*
70	*Egg Yolks*
300	*Thickened Cream (semi-whipped)*

2 *Sheets of Gelatine Leaves*

Method

1. Pre-soak gelatine in ice water. Once bloomed, squeeze to drain excess water. Place in a bowl and set aside at room temperature.

2. Heat milk and vanilla in a saucepan on the stove at medium heat.

3. At the same time, in a separate bowl use a hand whisk to beat egg yolks, cornflour and sugar vigorously until well combined. Be careful not to let this mixture boil.

4. Once the liquid in the saucepan is simmering, take off the heat and pour ½ into the egg yolks, cornflour and sugar mixture. Whisk with hand whisk until well incorporated.

5. Pour this mixture back into the saucepan with the other ½ of the liquid, and place back on the heat. Mix continuously using a rubber spatula until the mixture reaches 85°C. Then remove from the heat.

6. Pour mixture over gelatine, then blend with hand blender until smooth and glossy.

7. Pour into a cooled mixing bowl to bring the temperature down quickly. Then, put this in the fridge to bring the temperature down further to 40°C.

8. Fold through semi-whipped thickened cream using a rubber spatula.

9. Add to a piping bag when ready to use.

"all eyes on me"

To Assemble the Cake

1. Cut an acetate sheet to 38 cm by 15 cm.
2. Line a 12 cm cake ring with the acetate.
3. Strain the guinettes cherry and place the syrup into a squeeze bottle.
4. Place first chocolate *genoise* sponge disc at the bottom of the cake ring. With a fork, stab the sponge evenly all over.
5. Pour some cherry syrup over the sponge until well soaked.
6. Pipe vanilla cream around the outer edges of the sponge, then pipe some cherry jam at the centre of the sponge.
7. Place frozen *crémeux* in the middle of the sponge.
8. Pipe more vanilla cream to cover the *crémeux* until it is flush and even.
9. Place another sponge disc on top and repeat steps 4 to 8.
10. Place the final sponge disc, soak it in syrup and pipe vanilla cream over the top in an even layer.
11. Pipe cherry jam at the centre and freeze.
12. Spread tempered dark chocolate on to a stainless steel tray. Wait a few minutes until it's semi set. Use a scraper to scrape the spread chocolate to form chocolate cigarette rolls.
13. Once ready to use, remove cake from cake ring, take off the acetate and place candied cherries around the outer edge of the cake. Place some chocolate cigarette rolls in the middle. Decorate with gold leaves.

Chocolate Structure

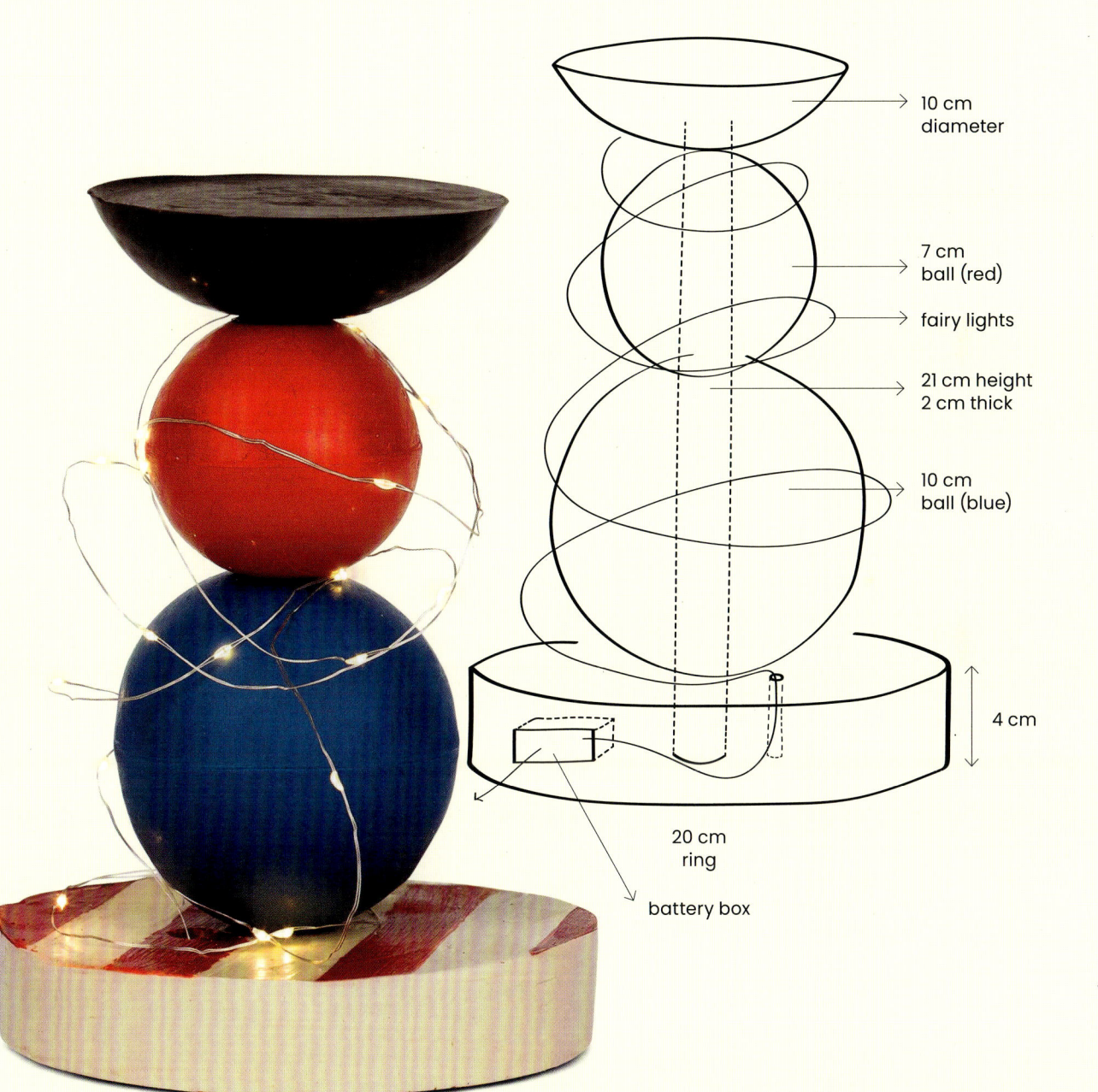

10 cm diameter

7 cm ball (red)

fairy lights

21 cm height
2 cm thick

10 cm ball (blue)

4 cm

20 cm ring

battery box

"all eyes on me"

To Assemble the Chocolate Structure

Ingredients

- Chocolate Velvet Blue Spray (readily available at baking stores)
- Chocolate Velvet Red Spray
- Gold Spray
- Cherry Guinette Decor (with stem)
- Gold Leaves or Flakes
- Cold Spray
- Tempered Dark Chocolate
- Tempered White Chocolate
- Liposoluble Red Colouring
- Liposoluble Blue Colouring

Equipment

- 20 cm Cake Silicon Mould
- 12 cm Cake Ring
- 18 cm Half-sphere Mould
- 10 inch Black Cake Board
- 10 cm Half-sphere Mould x 2
- 7 cm Half-sphere Mould x 2
- Round Cutter
- String Lights (I bought mine from Kmart, seriously)
- 1 inch diameter pvc Pipe (cut to 21 cm long)
- Knife
- 30 cm Stainless Steel Ruler
- Straw
- Masking Tape
- Cling Wrap (with wider width/commercial sized one)
- Squeeze Bottle
- 7 cm Cylinder Mould
- Tape Dispenser + Tape
- Frame Silicon Mould
- Chocolate Scraper

Method

1. Pour tempered dark chocolate into an 18 cm half-sphere mould, filling up ¼ of the mould. Place in the fridge to set.

2. Cut acetate into sheets measuring 10 cm by 24 cm, and line the inside of the pvc pipe. Wrap one side of the opening of the pvc pipe with cling wrap and place it vertically in a small jug, wrapped end down.

3. Pour tempered dark chocolate into the pipe until it reaches the top. Place the pipe (still upright in the jug) in the fridge to set.

4. Colour tempered white chocolate with red liposoluble colouring, then pour into 7 cm half-sphere mould. Wait a couple of minutes for it to harden on the outside, and then tip it upside down. Scrape excess chocolate that drips from the mould, leaving only the red shell behind. Place the mould upside down on a tray lined with baking paper, and place in the fridge to set.

5. Colour tempered white chocolate with blue liposoluble colouring, pour into 10 cm half-sphere mould. Wait a couple of minutes for it to harden on the outside, and then tip it upside down. Scrape excess chocolate that drips from the mould, leaving only the blue shell behind. Place the mould upside down on a tray lined with baking paper, and place in the fridge to set.

6. Measure the battery box, and build a box of the same size and shape using foam. Wrap the foam in cling wrap.

7. Place the 20 cm silicon round cake mould on to a tray.

8. Remove the chocolate tube from the fridge. Slide the hardened chocolate tube out of the pvc pipe, and peel off the acetate plastic.

9. Dip one end of the chocolate tube in tempered dark chocolate, and place it in the centre of the 20 cm silicon cake mould. Give it a cold spray to help it set immediately.

10   Halfway between the tube and the edge of the mould, place the wrapped foam box flat on the base of the mould.

11   Pour tempered white chocolate into the 20 cm mould, filling halfway. Give the surface of the white chocolate a cold spray to help it set immediately.

12   On the other side of the silicon cake mould, between the chocolate tube and the edge of the mould, stab in a paper straw, making sure it touches the base of the mould.

13   Pour more tempered white chocolate to fill the entire mould and to cover the foam box entirely. Lift the tray carefully and let the chocolate set completely in the fridge.

14   Unmould 2 blue and 2 red chocolate half-spheres. Place your smallest round cutter (around 2–3 cm in diameter) in hot water to warm it up, then cut a hole at the centre of each chocolate half-sphere by combining twisting movement and gentle pressure against the surface of chocolate. Don't use too much pressure: the warmth from the metal cutter would be more than enough to cut through the chocolate.

15   Run the flat side of each half-sphere on a warm tray and combine the half-spheres together, creating a red and a blue ball, each with a hole at each of the opposite sides.

16   Unmould the white chocolate base from the silicon cake mould, being careful not to break the chocolate tube.

17   At the bottom of the white chocolate base, the part that is touching the base of the silicon mould, one side of the wrapped foam box will be visible. Trace the tip of a knife around the box, and carefully pull out the box, leaving a square hollow cavity for the battery box.

18   On the other side of the mould, the end of the paper straw should be visible, too. With the tip off a knife, trace the hole of the straw and pull the straw out, leaving behind a small hole from the bottom of the white chocolate base to the top side of the base.

all eyes on me (cont'd)

advanced recipes

220

19 Cut some long strips of masking tape and wrap one around the side of the white chocolate base. Tape some strips on the top surface of the white chocolate base, making stripes.

20 Using the chocolate velvet red spray, spray the surface of the white chocolate base. Place in the fridge to let the red spray semi-set. Peel off the masking tape strips leaving behind red and white stripes on the top surface of the base.

21 Place the battery box in the cavity at the bottom of the white chocolate base, and thread the fairy lights through the small hole left by the paper straw from the bottom to the top of the base.

22 Thread the blue ball over the chocolate centre pole, followed by the smaller red ball. Using a knife dipped in hot water, cut any excess chocolate tube above the red ball, leaving just 2 mm of exposed tube at the top.

23 Unmould the dark chocolate in the 18 cm half-sphere mould.

24 Run the curved side of the dark chocolate on to a warm tray, and attach it to the exposed part of chocolate tube on top of the red ball. Cold spray it to set firmly, leaving the flat side at the top to be the base for your cherry sponge cake.

25 Wrap the fairy lights from the blue ball, all the way up to the red ball and the dark chocolate cake base. Flick on the battery switch to turn on the lights.

26 Carefully place the cake on the dark chocolate cake base. Add cherry decor and enjoy.

Green-y Smith Apple

This apple ... this humble apple ... I have contorted and twisted it beyond what you could ever dream. I've made it in all colours imaginable. Red, yellow, green, gold, white ... and black.

One thing about apples that I love is that their flavour is unmistakable, and somehow very bland and versatile at the same time. It's like a white canvas. I have used apple as a stabiliser in ice cream (because of its fibres), as a natural sweetener in *compote*, as a natural setter in jam, and as a background for flavours that otherwise would be so weird to put in dessert. Like black pepper. Hence, the black apple.

This is the original version of said apples. I hope you will twist it and adapt it, using the wildest parts of your imagination. Send me pictures when you do. Humble apples for the win!

Note: the given quantities will produce approximately 10–12 apples.

223

Lime & Vanilla *Ganache*

380	*Thickened Cream (A)*
170	*Lime Purée*
225	*White Chocolate*
380	*Thickened Cream (B)*

2 Sheets of Gelatine Leaves

Method

1. Pre-soak gelatine in ice water. Once bloomed, squeeze to drain excess water. Place in a bowl with the white chocolate.

2. Heat thickened cream (A), vanilla and lime *purée* in a saucepan on medium heat. Mix continuously with a rubber spatula until the mixture reaches 80°C.

3. Pour hot mixture over soaked gelatine and white chocolate, then blend with a hand blender until smooth and glossy.

4. Add thickened cream (B) and a hand blend to combine.

5. Cover with cling film, pressing down so that the cling film is touching the surface of the mixture. Refrigerate overnight.

6. Once set, whip to soft peaks with hand mixer, put in piping bag and set aside.

Apple *Compote*

500	Apples (peeled, sliced and brunois/chopped into cubes)
250	Lime Juice
225	Sugar
7	Pectin NH
QS	Vanilla
15	Dark Rum (optional)

Method

1. Take 50 g of sugar and put in a small bowl with pectin. Use a hand whisk to mix well. The sugar granules will break the pectin clumps.

2. In a saucepan on stove at medium heat, place ½ of the diced apples to cook until the outer side of the cubes are transparent, but the middle part is still white.

3. Pour in sugar and vanilla. Cook for another 5 minutes, mixing continuously using a rubber spatula.

4. Add the lime juice, dark rum (optional), the rest of the apples and the pectin and sugar mixture. Cook for another 5 minutes, then take off the heat and spread mixture onto a tray.

5. Place tray in the fridge to cool off.

6. Scoop the *compote* into 5 cm half-sphere moulds and place in freezer. Once frozen, unmould and store in the freezer until ready to use.

Caramel Milk Chocolate *Mousse*

75	*Sugar*
150	*Thickened Cream (A)*
60	*Egg Yolks*
350	*Milk Chocolate*
300	*Thickened Cream (B) (semi-whipped)*

2 *Sheets of Gelatine Leaves*

Method

1. Pre-soak gelatine in ice water. Once bloomed, squeeze to drain excess water. Place in a bowl together with milk chocolate, then set aside at room temperature.

2. Heat thickened cream (A), milk and vanilla in a saucepan on the stove at medium heat. Bring this to a simmer (don't let it boil!), then take off the heat. Set aside.

3. At the same time, in a separate saucepan caramelise the sugar on medium heat until it reaches a deep amber colour.

4. Pour warm cream, milk and vanilla mixture over the caramel to deglaze. Continue cooking mixture at low heat until all the caramel dissolves into the mixture.

5. Place egg yolks in a separate mixing bowl. Pour half the caramel liquid over the egg yolks and hand whisk until well incorporated. Pour this mixture back into the saucepan with the other half of the cream, milk and vanilla mixture, and place back on the stove.

6. Mix continuously using a rubber spatula until the mixture reaches 85°C. Then remove from the heat.

7. Immediately pour the hot mixture over the soaked gelatine and chocolate. Blend with a hand blender until smooth and glossy.

8. Pour into a cooled mixing bowl to bring the temperature down quickly. Then, put this in the fridge to bring the temperature down to 40°C.

9. Fold semi-whipped thickened cream (B) through the mixture using a rubber spatula.

10. Place *mousse* into a piping bag and pipe into 5 cm half-sphere moulds, then place in the freezer. Once frozen, unmould and store in the freezer until ready to use.

Spiced Milk Chocolate Crumble

125	Butter
125	Plain Flour
125	Almond Meal
63	Sugar
63	Brown Sugar
5	Salt
2.5	Cinnamon Powder
2.5	Nutmeg Powder
5	Ginger Powder
100	Milk Chocolate (melted)

Method

1. Preheat oven to 160°C (fan forced).

2. In a stand mixer bowl, use a paddle attachment to mix all ingredients (except for the milk chocolate) until well incorporated and a pliable dough is formed.

3. Line tray with a silicon mat. Place a wire rack on top of the tray and press dough through the wire rack to create even pieces. Remove the rack and distribute dough pieces evenly on the tray.

4. Place tray in oven for 15 minutes. Then, take tray out and use a metal scraper to scrape the pieces and roughly chop on tray.

5. Return the tray to the oven and bake for a further 15 minutes until pieces are golden brown in colour. If they're still pale, bake for another 5–10 minutes.

6. Cool crumble completely at room temperature.

7. Once cooled, fold in melted milk chocolate using spatula until all crumble pieces are well coated. Spread on to a tray and leave to cool at room temperature.

229

green-y smith apple

advanced recipes

Dipping Glaze (Green)

500	White Chocolate
165	Cocoa Butter
38	Vegetable Oil
QS	Green Liposoluble Food Colouring

Method

1. Melt cocoa butter in microwave at high setting in 30-second bursts.

2. Semi-melt white chocolate in microwave at high setting in 30-second bursts. Add melted cocoa butter and vegetable oil, then use a hand blender to mix until everything is well incorporated.

3. Add a tiny amount of green liposoluble food colouring and blend.

4. Set aside and keep warm inside the microwave with the door closed.

Green Shiny Glaze

114	*Milk*
232	*Pouring Cream*
230	*Sugar (A)*
80	*Glucose*
72	*Sugar (B)*
20	*Cornflour*
QS	*Green Hydrosoluble Food Colouring*
QS	*Gold Dust*
	2 Sheets of Gelatine Leaves

Method

1. Pre-soak gelatine in ice water. Once bloomed, drain excess water.

2. Heat milk, pouring cream, sugar and glucose in a saucepan on the stove at medium heat. Bring to a boil, mixing continuously with a rubber spatula. Once at a boil, take off heat.

3. In a separate small bowl, whisk sugar (B) and cornflour together to break the lumps. With a ladle, scoop some of the hot cream mixture into cornflour and sugar mixture and mix with a whisk until smooth and well combined.

4. Whisk cornflour slurry into hot cream mixture and bring back to a boil, mixing continuously with a rubber spatula.

5. Remove from the heat and add bloomed gelatine. Use a hand blender to mix everything until smooth.

6. Add green food colouring and gold dust to achieve desired colour.

7. Let the mixture cool in the fridge with cling film pressed down to touch the mixture surface all over.

8. To use, heat up glaze in microwave to 26°C, then use a hand blender to blend until smooth and even in temperature throughout.

green-y smith apple

Method

1 Warm a clean flat tray in the oven.

2 Run the bottom flat side of the caramel milk chocolate half-spheres to gently melt the surface. Attach frozen apple *compote* half-spheres to create a ball insert.

3 Place back in the freezer for 15 minutes.

4 Pipe whipped lime *ganache* into ¾ of the apple mould. Press the ball insert into the *ganache* and then cover with more *ganache*, leaving around 2 mm from the top of the mould (which is the base of the apple).

5 Sprinkle as much spiced crumble as possible on top of the mould to cover the 2 mm gap entirely. Use a palette knife to flatten the surface of the crumble and pack it into the apple.

6 Put the filled apple moulds in the freezer and leave overnight, or until completely frozen. Unmould and store in freezer until ready to decorate and finish.

7 Place milk chocolate buttons in a strong food processor and pulverise until a firm paste is formed. It should have a consistency similar to thick clay.

8   Place your hands in a tub of cold ice water, then dry completely. Take a small piece of the milk chocolate clay and roll on a cool work bench into an apple stalk shape. Set aside in the fridge until ready to use. (Tip: you can buy ready-made modeling chocolate and use it to create apple stalks instead of processing the milk chocolate).

9   Melt a small, equal amount of milk chocolate and cocoa butter in a microwave until completely melted.

10 Stick a skewer into the grooved top of the apple, then dip the entirety of the apple into green dipping chocolate.

11 Once dipping chocolate hardens on the apples, use a small soft brush dipped in the melted milk chocolate and cocoa butter mixture to brush the top and around the apples.

12 Dip the apples in the green shiny glaze quickly and lift up, letting some excess of glaze drip off. Place on a wire rack to allow more excess to drip off.

13 Place apples on boards, and quickly remove the skewers in a twisting motion.

14 Place the apple stalks into the holes where the skewers were.

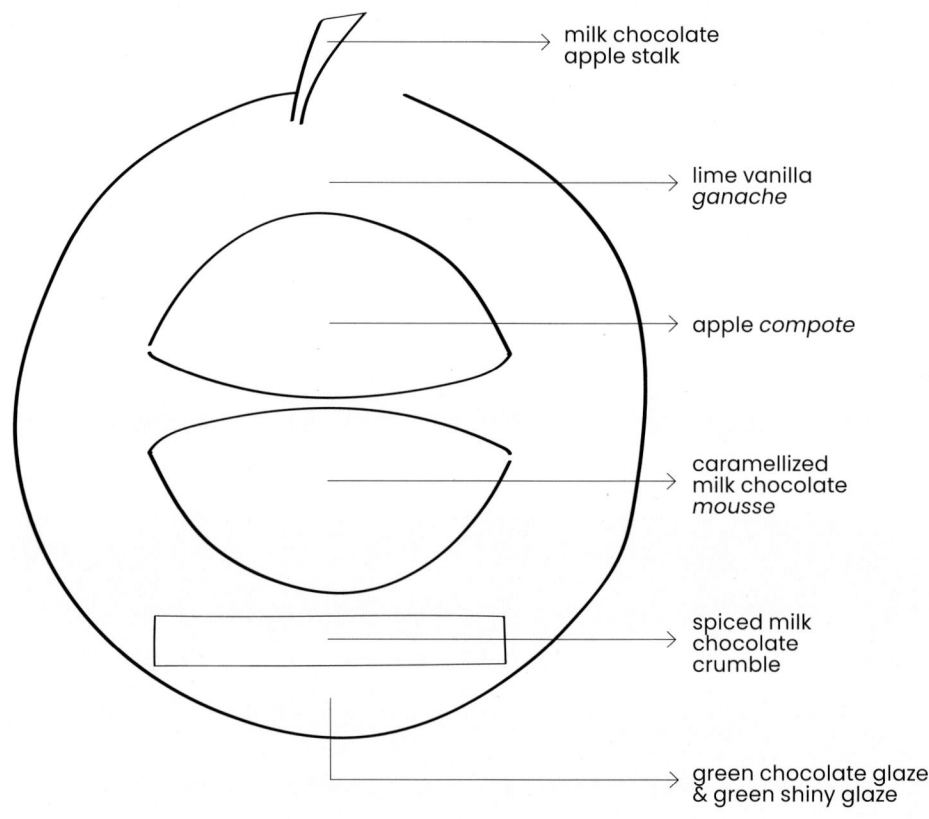

To Assemble the Apple

Ingredients

- Milk Chocolate *Couverture* (around 500 g)
- Cocoa Butter (around 100 g)

Equipment

- Small Brush
- Apple Moulds (you can buy these in baking supply stores)
- Strong Food Processor

237

What's Next

Thank you so much for allowing me to stimulate your dessert curiosity. When I started to write this book, my life revolved just around GLACÉ. Life got ... pretty boring, to be honest. But by the time I finished writing this book, I was a mother! I could drive! (Took me thirty-eight years to learn how to do that). I went on a nationally televised cooking competition and went all the way to Grand Finale (sorry! Spoiler!) after taking a hiatus of over twelve months. We renovated our original GLACÉ shop. I have so many exciting and incredible projects in the pipeline. It is *wild*.

Life has surprised me more than I could ever have imagined. I have become more capable than I could ever have imagined. But most importantly, life has reminded me to not be afraid to imagine. Life will challenge you, but will unfold in the most magical way.

The same goes with dessert making. Don't be afraid, and keep pushing. If you have a desire to be good at it, as a professional or amateur, your curiosity is as valuable as the amount of hours of practice you put on your hands.

All you have to do is imagine, and work towards making it a reality.

Much love,

Christy Tania

Published by Melbourne Books
Level 9, 100 Collins Street,
Melbourne, VIC 3000
Australia
www.melbournebooks.com.au
info@melbournebooks.com.au

Copyright © Christy Tania 2025
www.christytania.com.au

All rights reserved. No part of this publication may be reproduced, stored in a retrieval system, or transmitted in any form or any means electronic, mechanical, photocopying, recording or otherwise without the prior permission of the publisher.

No part of this book may be used or reproduced in any manner for the purpose of training artificial intelligence technologies or systems.

Title: Imagine: Creating Desserts with Christy Tania
Author: Christy Tania
ISBN: 9781922779427
Photography: Silvia Zanon, Atti.Co Melbourne
Videography: Michele Bonicelli, Atti.Co Melbourne
Design: Sarah Pistillo, Atti.Co Melbourne
Publisher: David Tenenbaum
Printed in China

 A catalogue record for this book is available from the National Library of Australia